Revelation Study Guide

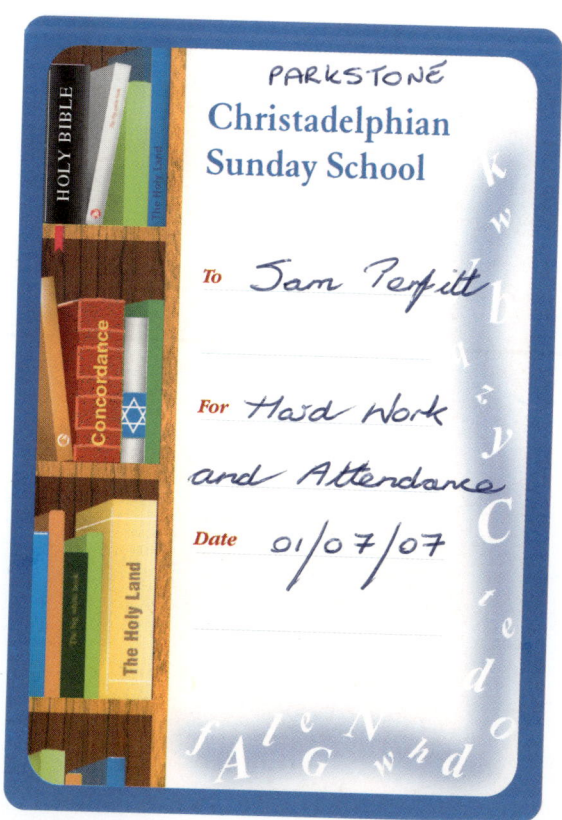

PARKSTONE
Christadelphian Sunday School

To Sam Perfitt

For Hard Work and Attendance

Date 01/07/07

Revelation
STUDY GUIDE

Michael Ashton

The Christadelphian
404 Shaftmoor Lane, Hall Green, Birmingham B28 8SZ, UK
©2007 The Christadelphian Magazine & Publishing Association Limited

First published 2007
ISBN 0 85189 173 X

Cover photograph:
The Isle of Patmos today

Printed in England by:
The Cromwell Press
TROWBRIDGE BA14 0XB

Contents

What is a Study Guide? vi

Preface vii

1. **Introduction**. 1
2. **The scheme of Revelation** 5
   The Old Testament Pattern
3. **A closer look** 7
   Seven clues
4. **Signs and symbols**. 11
5. **Sevenfold structure**. 13
   Leading to the great day of rest
6. **Visions of the kingdom**. 17
   The joy set before us
7. **Old Testament background** . . . 19
   Daniel and Zechariah
8. **Tale of two cities** 23
   Babylon and Jerusalem
9. **The development of the Beast** 27
   God's view of man's kingdom
10. **Corrupt religion** 33
    Believers facing greater tribulation
11. **Three great earthquakes**. 37
    Changes in world rulership
12. **Seven introductory letters** 39
13. **Time periods** 47
14. **Unsealing the scroll** 51
    Great changes in world government
15. **Seven trumpets** 57
    Calling nations to battle
16. **The witnesses**. 63
    Living through the second great earthquake
17. **More about the Beast** 67
    The religious dimension
18. **Seven last plagues** 73
    Judgements on the throne of the Beast
19. **Subduing the nations** 79
    Events during the Millennium
20. **New Heaven and New Earth** . . . 83
    God will be "all in all"

Further reading. 87

What is a Study Guide?

1. **Aims:** The overriding aim of all Bible study is that through knowledge and understanding of the word of God a person may become "wise unto salvation through faith which is in Christ Jesus" (2 Timothy 3:15).

   "Study Guides" are designed to explain the straightforward teachings of scripture and where appropriate to emphasise:

   a) First principles of doctrine
   b) Practical outcomes

   They should be helpful to young people, to those who are "young in the faith", who often have very little background knowledge of the scriptures, and to those of all ages and experience who enjoy straightforward, uncomplicated study of the Bible.

2. **Other features of Study Guides**

   a) **Layout:** After a brief introduction to the book, essential background information is provided before looking at the text in more detail. Headings and verse references make it easy to use the guide for looking up information on any section of the Bible text.

   b) **Bible versions:** This Guide mainly uses the New King James Version as a basis, as this helps to overcome problems of archaic expressions that exist in the Authorised (King James) Version (AV / KJV), which remains the most used translation in Christadelphian ecclesias today. Other versions can sometimes assist in clarifying a particular passage, but some popular modern versions are unreliable and betray the doctrinal bias of their translators.

   c) **Manageable sections:** Each Guide is divided into units of study which are not too long. This will make it easier for individuals or groups to make progress. An hour's concentrated and productive study on a regular basis is likely to yield good results.

   d) **Visual help:** The prophets and the Lord Jesus himself used visual illustrations to communicate their message. While the prime emphasis is on the written word, visual help is given wherever possible to increase understanding.

   e) **Use alongside the Bible:** The student must have a Bible open alongside the Guide.

   It is recommended at the outset that important information is marked in the Bible. Have a pencil at the ready.

   f) **Further study:** The final sections contain suggestions for further study and a book list chosen on the basis of sound expositional and doctrinal content.

   g) **Prayer:** We are studying the word of God. Before commencing any Bible study we must ask God's blessing on our activity. Thank God for making the Bible available to us, so that through it we may come to know Him and to look forward to His coming kingdom.

   Here is a prayer that sums up our aim:

   "Open thou mine eyes, that I may behold wondrous things out of thy law."
   (Psalm 119:18)

Preface

NEWCOMERS to the Bible often ask about the book of Revelation. There is something about its imagery that fascinates people of all ages. Yet there are good reasons for it being the last book in the Bible. First of all it contains the last recorded words of the Lord Jesus Christ. It places the final seal on the word of God, warning against all who might seek to add to its message, or take away from it.

Furthermore, it appears right at the end of the Bible because its message is very dependent on all that was written before, both in the Old Testament and in the New. The message completes the Gospel Jesus preached as he taught the people who lived in first century Israel, and it picks up and expands the teaching of the prophets who prepared the way for the appearance of the Son of God.

Jesus has promised to appear on earth again, and to set up on earth the kingdom of God. This great promise is the message of the book of Revelation, which explains in graphic terms the development of God's purpose following the death and resurrection of Jesus, and charting events that must occur before he returns. These lead unerringly to the time when the kingdom is established and God's name is honoured throughout the earth.

Down through the ages since the book was written, disciples of the Lord Jesus have found comfort and hope from his last message. They have joined with the Apostle John who first received it in crying out, *"Even so, come, Lord Jesus"* (Revelation 22:20).

The aim of this work is to open up the message of Revelation both for new readers and for those who are perplexed by its language and technique. In a short work like this, it is impossible to provide answers to every question, or comments on every verse. Those looking for more should consult some of the titles listed under the "Further reading" section. But if readers are encouraged to look more deeply into this fascinating message, and to wait patiently for its fulfilment, then the objective will have been met.

Jesus promised a blessing to all who read and keep his sayings, and he also promised to return and bestow God's blessings on an earth that will finally be free from sin and death. In reading his final message, we can prepare for that wonderful time.

MICHAEL ASHTON
Birmingham, January 2007

Acknowledgments

The publishers express their gratitude for the following photographs and illustrations:

- The Island of Patmos (front and rear covers), Alan Clarke.
- Jerusalem from the Mount of Olives (page 25), Roger Long.
- The statue of Diana of the Ephesians (page 33), David Wagner.
- The Illustration of Jericho (page 5); Nebuchadnezzar's image (pages 21, 27, 69); the beasts in Daniel 7 (pages 21, 69), Paul Wasson.
- All maps and other illustrations, Mark Norris (except on pages 19, 24, 53, 58, 78, which are from copyright-free sources).

Introduction

THE message of Revelation is daunting for anyone reading it for the first time. Because of the way it is presented, the book seems to conceal its message more than it reveals or uncovers it. Part of the difficulty is that the book of Revelation is different from all other New Testament books, and from most Old Testament books too. In the New Testament, the Gospels and Acts contain narrative accounts of events during the lifetime of Jesus and his disciples. The letters contain words of encouragement, advice and instruction. Revelation contains prophecy, but it is prophecy in a specialised form. There are some parts of the Old Testament written in the same style – Daniel and Zechariah, for example – and they can help to explain it.

A special language

To understand and appreciate the message of Revelation, it is necessary first of all to learn its special language and know how to view its pictures. For Revelation is primarily a book about **visions**. The Apostle John described what he saw, and what was revealed to him, but did not always explain exactly what the visions mean. Because this is a feature of the book of Revelation (Greek, *apokalupsis*), the experts call it 'apocalyptic' literature. It contains visions of angels, beasts, living creatures, horsemen and fabulous armies, rainbows and stars, thunders, lightning and great earthquakes.

This book is designed to help new readers find their way round the book of Revelation and understand some of the images and language it uses. It deliberately refrains from getting into too much detail, in the hope that the overall message will be more easily understood. There are other books available that explain Revelation in more detail; information on these can be found in "Further reading" on page 87.

A message for Jesus' servants

Revelation is Jesus' last message, given to his "servants" and those who wish to be his servants. The message is important and exciting, and it is hoped that by means of this short work something of the enjoyment it imparts will be conveyed to readers.

Discovering who these servants are will also explain where the message is set. If, like many prophecies in the Old Testament, the book was addressed primarily to Jews, the message is likely to concentrate on incidents involving the nation or territory of Israel.

REVELATION STUDY GUIDE

But it is soon apparent that the book is addressed to believers in the Lord Jesus Christ, irrespective of their nationality. And the opening section, containing letters to groups of believers in different cities in the Roman province of Asia, suggests that these servants of Jesus were central to the book's setting.

The geographical setting

As a message for Jesus' servants, Revelation concerns the geographical area they inhabited. We are not left in any doubt where this was, for the New Testament faithfully records the spread of the Gospel from its earliest beginnings in Jerusalem until there were believers in the heart of the Roman Empire. Any map showing the spread of Christianity in the centuries immediately after Christ depicts the stage on which the visions of Revelation are acted out.

Who wrote Revelation?

The message itself is from the Lord Jesus Christ, as the first verse explains – *"The Revelation of Jesus Christ"*. But Jesus received it **from** his Father, the Lord God, for *"God gave (it) him"*. It was given *"to show his servants things which must shortly take place"*, and it was conveyed *"by his (i.e., Jesus') angel to his servant John"*.

What was passed by these means was *"the word of God"* and *"the testimony of Jesus Christ"* (verse 2). The Apostle John, who received the message, *"was on the island that is called Patmos for the word of God and for the testimony of Jesus Christ"* (verse 9). Patmos is a small island in the Aegean Sea, off the coast of modern Turkey (see maps alongside). In those days the Turkish peninsula was the Roman province known as Asia, and the island of Patmos was used by Rome to house political exiles.

Like the Apostle Paul before him, John felt that he was *"the prisoner of the Lord"*

"You shall be witnesses to me in Jerusalem, and in all Judea and Samaria, and to the end of the earth." (Acts 1:8)

As the Gospel spread outwards from Jerusalem, the apostles preached eventually in Rome, the Empire's capital city. In exile on the island of Patmos, the Apostle John was geographically close to the centre of this great development.

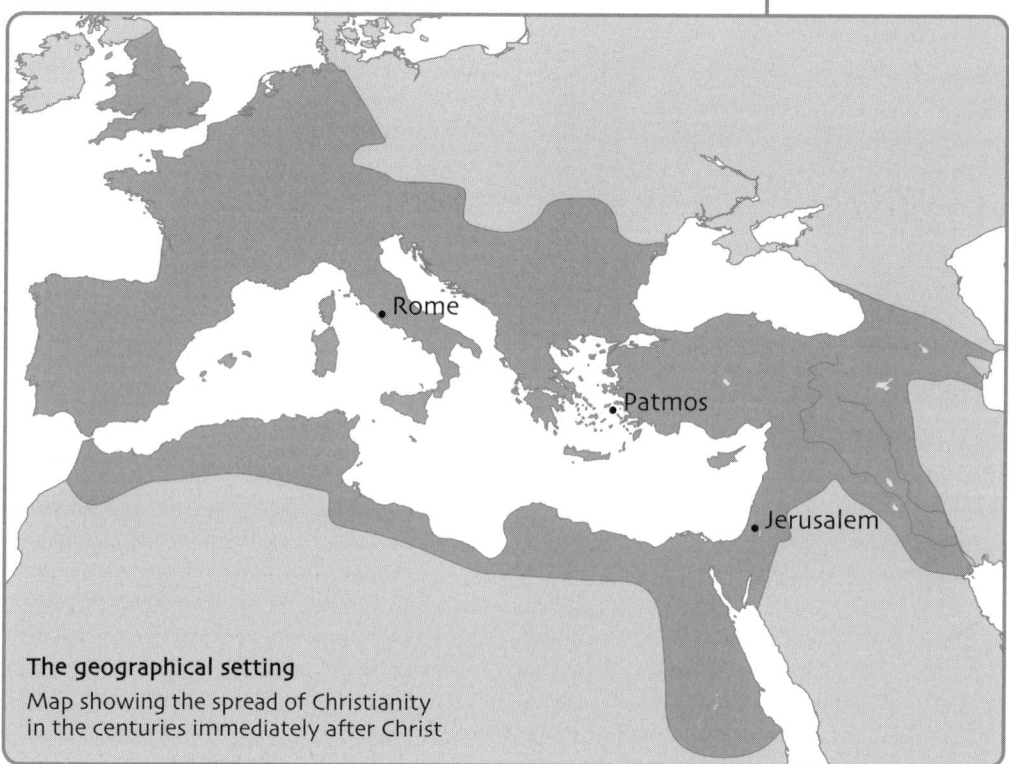

The geographical setting
Map showing the spread of Christianity in the centuries immediately after Christ

INTRODUCTION

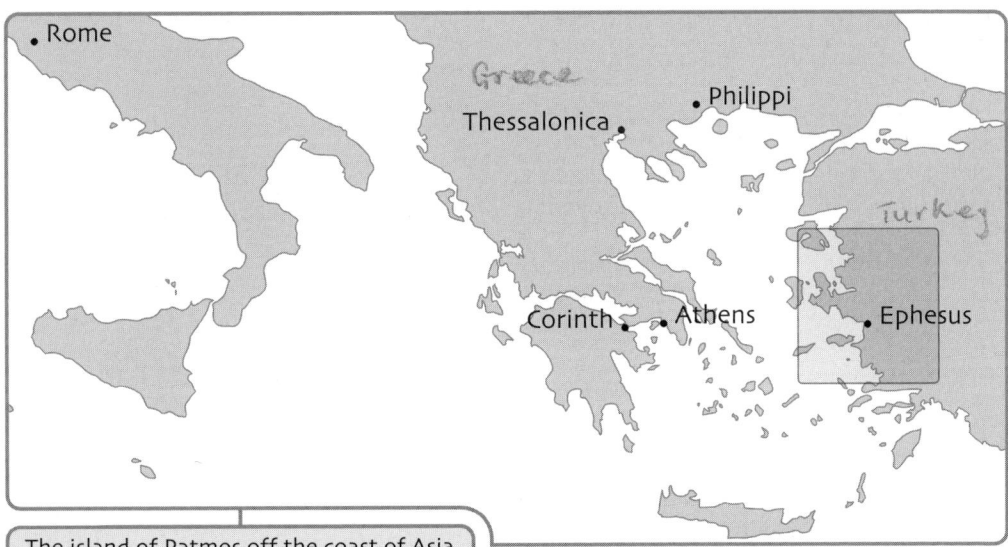

The island of Patmos off the coast of Asia

rather than the prisoner of the Roman emperor (cp. Ephesians 4:1), and that he was in Patmos for the express purpose of receiving this message from Jesus.

The Apostle John

John was one of the disciples chosen by Jesus to accompany him during his ministry. He was originally a fisherman from Galilee; son of Zebedee, and brother of James. These two brothers, together with Simon Peter, were the disciples chosen by Jesus to be with him on special occasions during his ministry – e.g., the transfiguration, and when Jairus' daughter was raised from the dead. After Peter and James died for their faith, it was appropriate that John, the last survivor of the inner group of Jesus' disciples, should receive the message of Revelation directly from Jesus.

When was Revelation written?

As John was imprisoned on Patmos for his faith, the Revelation must have been received from Jesus during a period of religious persecution. In John's lifetime there were two such periods: in the reigns of Nero (AD54-68) and Domitian (AD81-96). The evidence of most early writers points to the later period as the time when John was exiled and Revelation was written.

Some commentators rely completely on the earlier date, and apply the message of the book to the fall of Jerusalem in AD70. But the date of writing cannot be used to prove the book's teaching. It is sufficient for us to know that all the New Testament books were completed by the end of the first century AD, and were written when Rome was the leading world power.

Things which must shortly take place

Another factor that can easily cause us to misunderstand the message of Revelation is to miss the importance of the first verse:

> "The Revelation of Jesus Christ, which God gave him to show his servants – things which must shortly take place. And he sent and signified it by his angel to his servant John."

We have seen how this explains that the message originated with God, and was passed first to Jesus, then by Jesus' angel to John who recorded it for the benefit of the followers of Jesus. The message took the form of visions and prophetical signs, rather than direct descriptions of future events.

But this verse also explains the content of the message: it is about *"things which must shortly take place"* (see also 22:6). It does not review events that occurred before John was exiled in Patmos: we have to go elsewhere in the Bible to find those mentioned.

Whatever we read in Revelation must therefore refer to incidents that all still lay in the future for the Apostle *John*, and starting with conditions that were familiar to him. The conclusion we shall come to is that he *was shown the development of God's purpose* from his own times (c. AD 100), right through to the time when Jesus will return to establish God's kingdom … and beyond – *a vast panorama of the history of mankind, seen from the divine viewpoint.*

The events John was shown were selected ones; they are the important events involving the disciples of Jesus and the situations they faced. John was to bear witness to these incidents, which he described as *"the testimony of* (or, about) *Jesus Christ"* (verse 2). A verse later in Revelation explains that this was the basis of selection for the events included in the visions that John saw. *"The testimony of Jesus is the spirit of prophecy"* (19:10): i.e., the things concerning Jesus and his work are the motivation of the prophecy contained in the book of Revelation.

The Lord's day

This is confirmed in chapter 1, where John says he received the message when he *"was in the Spirit on the Lord's Day"* (verse 10). Whenever it is mentioned in the Bible, *"the day of the LORD"* refers to God intervening in the affairs of mankind to move events towards their foreordained conclusion. In contemplating this final Great Day of the Lord, John was well prepared to receive the message of Revelation from the Lord Jesus Christ.

If we are to understand the message of the book, we shall need a clear picture to guide us. An incident in the early history of the nation of Israel provides a model to help understand both the message of Revelation and how it is presented. This is the subject of the next chapter.

Methods of Interpretation

The Book of Revelation has always fascinated Bible students, and many attempts have been made to understand its message. Vastly different methods of interpretation have been used at different times. These can be briefly summarised as fitting into one of three main approaches:

➤ **FUTURIST:** this method sees the book as a description of the events immediately surrounding the return of the Lord Jesus Christ, probably all occurring during a period of intense activity lasting three-and-a-half years.

➤ **PRETERIST:** this approach views much of the material as referring to events occurring around the lifetime of the Apostle John (from Latin, *praeter*, past).

➤ **HISTORIC:** this view sees Revelation filling in details of significant events that affect believers, starting in John's day and continuing until Jesus returns. For the reasons given alongside, this is the approach followed in this Study Guide.

The scheme of Revelation

THE OLD TESTAMENT PATTERN

WHEN the children of Israel were about to enter the land of promise under the leadership of Joshua, they came across highly fortified cities that had to be captured and destroyed. Jericho was the first city to be attacked and taken. Under God's instructions the Israelites learned how the city could be captured without the use of warfare. God's instructions were simple:

> "You shall march around the city, all you men of war; you shall go all around the city once. This you shall do six days. And seven priests shall bear seven trumpets of rams' horns before the ark. But the seventh day you shall march around the city seven times, and the priests shall blow the trumpets. It shall come to pass, when they make a long blast with the ram's horn, and when you hear the sound of the trumpet, that all the people shall shout with a great shout; then the wall of the city will fall down flat. And the people shall go up every man straight before him."
> (Joshua 6:3-5)

An acted parable

This real-life incident was like an acted parable of the purpose of God:

- Jericho, where God was not recognised or worshipped, represents the kingdom of men in its opposition to God.
- Joshua represents the Lord Jesus Christ (the Hebrew name 'Joshua' becomes 'Jesus' in Greek). He who saves
- The Israelites represent the people of God.
- The priests with trumpets represent God's angels who fulfil His will.
- The outcome is the destruction of the kingdom of men and the establishment of the kingdom of God.

If we can remember how Jericho was destroyed, we can explain the message of Revelation. It is summed up in the following important verse:

> "The kingdoms of this world have become the kingdoms of our Lord and of his Christ, and he shall reign for ever and ever!" (Revelation 11:15)

In addition to the overall picture presented by the account of the destruction of Jericho, some of its details reappear in Revelation. As the people marched round the city once a day for six days, and for seven times on the seventh day, so the book of Revelation is divided into separate sequences of 'sevens'. Each seventh section contains the next 'seven', and so on. We can call this a 'Jericho pattern'.

John is shown a seven-sealed scroll. Six seals are opened in turn. When the seventh seal is opened, seven angel trumpeters are revealed. Six of these trumpets are sounded, one after another. When the seventh trumpet sounds, seven bowls or plagues are poured out one at a time, and the seventh bowl is seen to contain seven thunders. Only when all these things have happened is the kingdom of men overthrown and replaced by the kingdom of God.

Destroyed and devoted

God commanded that everything to do with Jericho had to be completely destroyed; nothing was to be left. The Israelites were given strict instructions not to take any plunder from the city – everything was to be devoted to God; the people were killed and the city was burned.

When the kingdom of God replaces the kingdom of men, the same will be true. After the work of Jesus and the saints during the Millennium – his thousand-year reign on earth – nothing of man's rule will be left: *"For the earth will be filled with the knowledge of the glory of the LORD, as the waters cover the sea"* (Habakkuk 2:14).

Not quite everything in Jericho was destroyed. Despite living in that heathen city, one woman – Rahab the harlot – and her family believed in God. By showing faith in Him and trusting the word of the two Israelites who spied out the city, Rahab's family was saved. Although she lived in Jericho, Rahab chose not to be part of Jericho. She was asked to hang a scarlet rope from the window of her house, and that part of Jericho was left standing when everything else was flattened.

This is the message of Revelation. It explains about the destruction of the kingdom of men, but contains a great message of hope for the faithful who will be saved. They are not saved by a scarlet thread, *"but with the precious blood of Christ, as of a lamb without blemish and without spot"* (1 Peter 1:19). This is described in Revelation as follows:

> *"From Jesus Christ, the faithful witness, the firstborn from the dead, and the ruler over the kings of the earth. To him who loved us and washed us from our sins in his own blood, and has made us kings and priests to his God and Father, to him be glory and dominion forever and ever. Amen."* (Revelation 1:5,6)

The next step

Together with this picture of the overall theme of Revelation, we shall also need some clues to follow if we are to understand some of the details of its message. The next chapter provides seven of these as we take a closer look at Revelation.

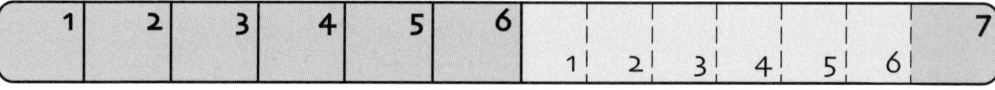

The Jericho Pattern

A closer look

SEVEN CLUES

Seven clues

- Sevenfold structure
- Visions of the kingdom
- Old Testament background
- A tale of two cities
- The development of the Beast
- Corrupt religion
- Three great earthquakes

THE seven clues listed alongside are designed to introduce the message of Revelation. They do not explain everything the book contains, but they will help new readers begin to find their way around.

From the example of the destruction of Jericho, we have already seen the importance of the sequence of 'sevens', but there are other clues too.

1 – Sevenfold structure

The pattern first used at Jericho is more complicated when it appears in Revelation. It is not just one series of seven containing another seven, but a whole sequence of sevens containing other sevens. The seven seals open out into seven trumpets, the seventh trumpet introduces seven plagues, and the seven plagues contain seven thunders. As a result of all these events, the city of man (i.e., human civilisation) falls into the hands of Christ and his followers.

In each phase, the last part of the sequence (the seventh) leads directly to God's kingdom being established. One of the effects of the successive sevenfold sequences is that more detail is provided as God's plan unfolds, increasing in intensity as the final fulfilment approaches. This is important for us, as we live in the years close to Christ's return.

2 – Visions of the kingdom

The book of Revelation pictures the incidents and events that lead towards the establishing of the kingdom of God. As we have already considered, each section ends with the kingdom. But, in order to keep this objective to the forefront at all times, each sequence of activity is also introduced by a vision of the kingdom to which those events will lead.

Before the seven-sealed scroll is opened, for example, there is a vision of a Lamb *"as though it had been slain"* standing before God's throne with a great company of people worshipping and saying: *"Worthy is the Lamb who was slain to receive power and riches and wisdom, and strength and honour and glory and blessing!"* (5:12).

This is a picture of Jesus when God gives him all rule, authority and power to set up His kingdom on earth. The section that follows the vision in Revelation describes the events leading up to Jesus' return, and culminates in all that John saw in that vision. These events are shown as if they are written on a scroll, with each successive section being opened and made visible when its seal is broken.

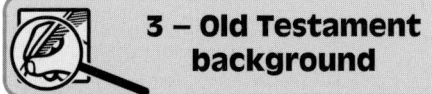

3 – Old Testament background

We started our study of Revelation by looking at the Old Testament account of the destruction of Jericho. Throughout our consideration of its message, we shall need to refer to the Old Testament background. The prophecy of Daniel is particularly helpful.

Like the Apostle John, the prophet Daniel was shown in a vision how the kingdom of God would replace the kingdom of men. Revelation fills out some of the details, where the prophecy of Daniel often sketches just the general outline.

Because some information already appears in the book of Daniel, some of the symbols in Revelation are not explained in its pages; we often need to turn back to Daniel and other scriptures to find the key. It is therefore very useful to become familiar with the sections of Daniel's prophecy that record the unfolding history of God's dealings with the kingdom of men (Daniel chapters 2, 7, 8 and 11).

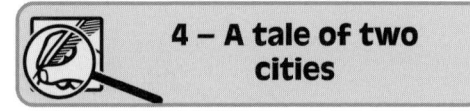

4 – A tale of two cities

Revelation contrasts two different cities, Jerusalem and Babylon. Both are symbolic cities, and we shall understand the symbols more easily if we discover information about the original historical cities.

Throughout the Bible, Babylon stands for a civilisation founded on false worship. By contrast, Jerusalem was the city chosen by God as the site of the temple where He was to be worshipped in truth. In Revelation, therefore, Babylon and Jerusalem identify religious systems and powers with different motivations and different destinies.

Babylon is shown to be wholly concerned with human power and government; and in the end it is to be utterly destroyed: *"With violence the great city Babylon shall be thrown down, and shall not be found any more"* (18:21).

By contrast, *"New"* Jerusalem is produced by God through the work of Jesus Christ, and is *"prepared as a bride adorned for her husband"* (21:2).

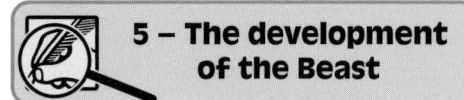

5 – The development of the Beast

The city and kingdom of men is shown pictorially in Revelation by a succession of beasts who seek to control and destroy the followers of Jesus. We shall discover that there is really only one Beast, changing in character as events proceed but having the same basic outlook. The development of this Beast, sometimes referred to in Revelation as "the Devil" or "the Serpent" because of its evil character, is both fascinating and terrifying.

We shall discover that the Beast in Revelation is the same Beast that Daniel saw in his visions, and described by him as *"dreadful and terrible, exceedingly strong. It had huge iron teeth; it was devouring, breaking in pieces, and trampling the residue* (i.e., of God's people) *with its feet"* (Daniel 7:7).

6 – Corrupt religion

Another development is also described in Revelation. While the Beast's power is shown to grow and change, important developments take place among the followers of Jesus.

After the passing of the apostles, and because of persecutions and attacks on their beliefs, Jesus' followers come under severe pressure. Some of them remain true to their calling, and as Rahab was saved when Jericho was destroyed, God also preserves these followers of Jesus through every persecution. Finally, they are given a part in His kingdom. They are *"called, chosen, and faithful"* (17:14), and are described by a variety of different terms:

- witnesses;
- the Woman's seed;
- the saints;
- those who hold the testimony of Jesus Christ.

But there are others who, under many different influences, gradually forsake some of the Lord's teachings. Over a period of time, the gospel they preach becomes different from the one preached by Jesus and his apostles. They make accommodations with political leaders and the society of their day, flirting with the powers of the age like a prostitute offering her favours.

This is the image presented in Revelation of many who started to follow Jesus. He looked for a chaste virgin (2 Corinthians 11:2), but many who claimed to be Christians were like a *"great harlot"* (Revelation 17:1).

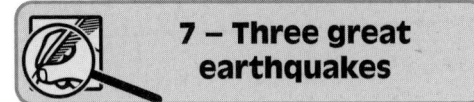

7 – Three great earthquakes

Punctuating the record of God's developing purpose are three *"great earthquakes"*. These use the symbol of a natural phenomenon to describe important incidents of sudden and decisive change in the affairs of mankind, when God *"shakes the heavens and the earth"* (i.e., the governments and peoples of all nations). These three great earthquakes occur:

- during the sixth seal period;
- after the sixth trumpet is blown;

- when the seventh and last plague is poured out.

The earthquakes reinforce the importance of these different sections. The third, last and greatest earthquake – the mightiest there has ever been – occurs when *"great Babylon was remembered before God"*, and the time of her destruction was near (16:19).

The Old Testament prophet Zechariah also spoke of this last great earthquake when he was prophesying about the glorious return to the earth of Jesus (Zechariah 14:4,5). It seems from Zechariah that this final, political upheaval will be accompanied by a literal earthquake or earthquakes, destroying the kingdom of men, and replacing it by the kingdom of God.

If we remember these seven clues as we read Revelation, many of the difficulties created by its different and unusual style will soon disappear. We shall find that the use of pictures and symbols will illuminate the message, and not cloud it.

To provide an early key to help decipher their meanings, the next chapter will specifically consider the use of signs and symbols in Revelation.

Breakdown of Revelation, chapter by chapter

1:1-8	Introduction
1:9-20	Vision of man among lampstands
2:1-3:22	Seven letters
4:1-5:14	Vision of throne in heaven and the Lamb
6:1-17	Six seals
7:1-8:5	Vision of multitude no man can number
8:6-9:21	Six trumpets
10:1-11	Vision of rainbowed angel
11:1-14	Two witnesses
11:15-19	The seventh trumpet
12:1-17	The Woman and her child
13:1-18	The Beast
14:1-20	Vision of the redeemed with the Lamb on Mount Zion
15:1-8	Vision of final judgements
16:1-21	Seven plagues
17:1-18:24	Judgement of the great Babylonian Harlot
19:1-10	Vision of the Lamb's Bride
19:11-21	Victory over the Beast
20:1-15	Subduing the nations
21:1-22:21	Vision of new heaven and new earth

Signs and symbols

THROUGHOUT the book of Revelation there is extensive use of symbolic and figurative language. Initially, this is what makes the book so difficult to understand.

Yet the message is from the Lord Jesus Christ, and claims to uncover future events, not to conceal them. We are reminded of Jesus' use of parables during his earthly ministry. He said to his disciples: *"I speak to them* (i.e., the people) *in parables, because seeing they do not see, and hearing they do not hear, nor do they understand ... For the hearts of this people have grown dull. Their ears are hard of hearing, and their eyes they have closed ... But blessed are your eyes for they see, and your ears for they hear"* (Matthew 13:13-16).

Ears to hear

The way prophecy is presented in Revelation therefore makes the message obscure to those who have closed their eyes, ears and hearts, but *"He who has ears to hear, let him hear!"* (verse 9, cp. Revelation 2:7,11,17 etc.).

For this reason, Jesus promises a blessing to those who hear: *"Blessed is he who reads and those who hear the words of this prophecy, and keep those things which are written in it; for the time is near"* (Revelation 1:3).

Jesus' parables are actually a very good introduction to his use of signs and symbols in Revelation. We are familiar with the parable of the sower, for example, where the seed is *"the word of the kingdom"*, the different ground conditions refer to the responses of various individuals, and thorns and thistles represent the cares of the world, etc. The Gospel message is not literally preached by sowing seed in a field, but it is a very graphic way of describing the process of how people receive and respond to God's word.

Jesus explained to his disciples the meaning of the various symbols in his parables. The same is true in Revelation. Keys to the meanings of the various symbols can be found, sometimes within Revelation itself, but often elsewhere in the Bible. To understand its message, we therefore need to be reasonably familiar with the rest of the Bible.

Clashing symbols

Understanding another important principle about the symbols in Revelation will also help to explain Jesus' message. Most of the symbols can be grouped in contrasting pairs; they represent something that can develop in either a Godly way or a worldly way. There is, for example, the symbol of a woman, and this is used to represent a religious community.

As this symbol develops throughout Revelation, we discover that one *"woman"* becomes a fallen woman – a prostitute. She represents those people who do not remain faithful to Jesus, but distort, corrupt, and pervert his teaching.

Thankfully there is also another *"woman"*, and she does remain faithful, despite terrible persecutions and trials. She prepares herself for the great day when she will marry her Lord.

The symbols in Revelation are therefore often 'clashing' symbols. Though they start in the same way, they develop in different directions until they are directly in opposition to each other.

The list alongside shows what some of the symbols represent. The list is not exhaustive, but it is provided at this point as a reference as you read through the book. Explanations of some of these symbols appear later, together with appropriate scripture references.

Some symbols and their meanings

Symbol	Meaning
Lampstand	Congregation of believers
Two-edged sword	Word of God
White robes	Righteousness
Burnished brass	Man's nature perfected
Heaven	Government
Earth	Peoples
Sea	All nations
Living creatures	Saints
Elders	Saints
Lion of Judah	Jesus as King
Lamb	Jesus as Saviour
Horse	Military power
Altar	Jesus' sacrifice
Earthquake	Political upheaval
Sun	King or emperor
Moon	Religious powers, priesthood
Stars	Princes, rulers
Trumpets	Judgements to come
Censer	Prayers
Rainbow	God's glorious covenant
Temple	Jesus and his faithful disciples
Court	Those who claim to be Christ's
Bottomless pit	Out of bounds
Woman	Religious community

Sevenfold structure

LEADING TO THE GREAT DAY OF REST

Sevens in Revelation

- **7** churches
- **7** spirits
- **7** golden candlesticks
- **7** stars
- **7** lamps of fire
- **7** seals on a scroll
- **7** horns and **7** eyes on the Lamb
- **7** angels with **7** trumpets
- **7** thunders
- **7** heads with **7** crowns on the Dragon
- **7** angels with **7** bowls containing the **7** last plagues
- **7** mountains and **7** kings
- **7** blessings

THE number seven is closely interwoven into the book of Revelation. We have already considered from the example of Jericho how one set of 'sevens' can contain another. But as well as determining the structure of the book, there are lots of other 'sevens' to be found in Revelation (a list of some of them is set out alongside).

The Sabbath

Seven is an important number in the Bible. It is always associated with the power of God in creation, and with the completion of His work, *"For in six days the LORD made the heavens and the earth, the sea, and all that is in them, and rested the seventh day. Therefore the LORD blessed the Sabbath day and hallowed it"* (Exodus 20:11).

The seventh day of the Israelite's week became a day of rest and worship, and taught about God's intention to fill the earth with His glory. As the writer to the Hebrews said, *"There remaineth therefore a sabbath rest for the people of God"* (Hebrews 4:9, RV).

The Year of Release

In the Israelites' calendar, the seven-day week was just the start of how the number seven affected everyday life. Each year, the Jews celebrated a Feast of Weeks (or Pentecost, meaning fiftieth, i.e., seven 'sevens'). These seven weeks marked the period between the first fruit of barley harvest and the full harvest.

Every seventh year, the land was left to lie fallow, requiring God's people to rely on Him completely. This Year of Release was also an opportunity to show generosity and to remove the burden of debt and slavery.

Jubilee

As the weekly Sabbath extended to the Feast of Weeks, the Year of Release also extended to a period of seven times seven years. After every 49 years a Jubilee was celebrated: a year of joy and rejoicing, when trumpets were blown and God's abundant goodness was commemorated with much festivity.

The sevenfold pattern thus formed part of everyday life in Bible times: seven days, seven weeks, seven years, and finally seven times seven years. On each occasion, the faithful man or woman in Israel was reminded of God's love and care, and of the great Day of Rest when the kingdom will be established.

If the seven-day week was to remind Israel of God's purpose and His ways, the constantly repeated 'sevens' in the book of Revelation remind readers that His purpose

The Jericho pattern

At the heart of the message in Revelation there are three sequences of sevens: seven seals, seven trumpets, and seven last plagues. The seventh seal opens up into the seven trumpets; and the seventh trumpet sounds the start of the seven plagues. These great sequences of important events divide into three successive sections the period of time between John receiving the message of Revelation and Jesus returning to earth to establish the kingdom.

This central section of Revelation mainly explains forthcoming political events. There are also religious events, and these are explained separately.

We shall need to refer to this threefold division on a number of occasions as we work our way through Revelation. The diagram below shows the relationship between the three sequences of sevens. Further details will be added as we move into later chapters. It is sufficient at this stage for us to see how the 'Jericho-pattern', as we might call it, is used to present the information in Revelation.

Seven sections

The whole book of Revelation can also be divided into seven parts, each having an opening vision (a cameo or snapshot of the kingdom), and each capable of being subdivided into seven parts. These seven main divisions are shown opposite. We shall look at their subdivisions later.

The three main periods described in Revelation

Seals		1	2	3	4	5	6	7												
Trumpets								1	2	3	4	5	6	7						Kingdom
Plagues													1	2	3	4	5	6	7	

SEVENFOLD STRUCTURE

But, as with the 'sevens' in Israel's calendar, and the sevenfold judgement on Jericho, the final – or 'seventh' – incident is always being anticipated. The labourer waited eagerly for the day of rest; debtors and slaves looked forward to the Year of Release; the nation made plans to celebrate the Jubilee; and the children of Israel had faith that Jericho would be destroyed to allow them to enter the promised land.

Opening visions

In Revelation too, each sevenfold sequence always looks forward to the completion of God's purpose. This is emphasised by the fact that every section starts with a vision of the kingdom, and is completed only when the kingdom is established. The vital importance of the kingdom visions is therefore our next subject.

The sevenfold construction of Revelation

	Opening Vision	Developments in God's Purpose
1	One like the Son of Man (Chapter 1)	Letters to the Seven Ecclesias in Asia (Chapters 2 & 3)
2	Throne in Heaven (Chapters 4 & 5)	Seven-sealed Scroll (Chapter 6)
3	Multitude no man can number (Chapter 7)	Seven Trumpets (Chapters 8 & 9)
4	Rainbowed Angel (Chapter 10)	Development of Apostasy (Chapters 11-13, 17, 18)
5	Lamb on Mount Zion (Chapter 14)	Seven Last Plagues (Chapter 16)
6	God's Judgements (Chapter 15)	Seven Thunders (Chapter 10:3,4)
7	Marriage of the Lamb (Chapter 19)	Establishment of the Kingdom (Chapters 20-22)

REVELATION STUDY GUIDE

Visions of the kingdom

THE JOY SET BEFORE US

WHATEVER part of Revelation we are reading, the kingdom is never far away. The book starts and finishes with pictures of the kingdom, and there are other visions of the kingdom at many different stages throughout the book. The kingdom is therefore the centre and focus of the whole book. Through the different visions of the kingdom we are given a lot of detailed information about the future age, and of the part faithful believers will play when God's glorious character will be manifested throughout the earth.

This is the final stage in God's purpose with His creation. Jesus' work ensured that men and women can hope to share in the glories of the future age. So his final message is a great encouragement to all who believe in him. His disciples are encouraged to follow the example of Jesus, *"who for the joy that was set before him endured the cross, despising the shame"* (Hebrews 12:2). In these visions of the kingdom, the same joy is being set before us to help us endure temptation and trials.

The visions generally introduce a new section of Revelation, and set the scene for what follows. Jesus starts each section by showing John a picture of the kingdom age, and then he reveals to him what has to happen before those conditions can exist. One way we can understand this method of presentation is to think of a set of instructions for a construction kit.

A completed kit of parts

The outside of the box always shows a picture of the completed model – this is like the vision of the kingdom. Inside the box are the step-by-step instructions – they are like the sections that follow the kingdom visions.

Naturally there is a strong relationship between the picture of the completed model and the instructions. In the same way, the special aspects of the kingdom visions are appropriate to the particular sections they introduce. The various kingdom visions are summarised on the next page, showing how they are related to the sections that follow.

A fuller understanding of the kingdom gradually emerges by this method. We are shown how God's glory will eventually fill the earth *"as the waters fill the seas"*.

Seven kingdom visions

Vision 1 – One like the Son of Man (1:12-20)

A symbolical figure representing Jesus and his faithful disciples encourages John to write down everything he is shown in the vision.

This kingdom vision introduces the letters to seven groups of believers in the province of Asia, and they describe the qualities God looks for in His people – those who will finally be united with Jesus when he returns.

Vision 2 – Throne in heaven (4:1 – 5:14)

A vision of Jesus sitting on God's throne in the kingdom. The nations are at peace, and the saints surround Jesus. Jesus holds a scroll sealed with seven seals; no one can open it, except a slain Lamb.

This vision explains how God foresees future events, and that they occur only at His will. Whatever happens, everything is moving towards the end of His purpose when Jesus will be enthroned in glory. As the seven seals are broken, some of these details are revealed.

Vision 3 – Multitude no man can number (7:9-17)

A great crowd of people from every nation stand before Jesus' kingdom throne. They are all clothed in white after coming through great tribulation and persecution.

This is a fitting introduction to the section where seven trumpet judgements are described. These reveal the troubles through which God's faithful people are preserved for His kingdom.

Vision 4 – Rainbowed angel (10:1-11)

A mighty angel descends from heaven, clothed in a cloud and a rainbow, and roaring like a lion. It is a vision of Jesus and the saints establishing peace on the earth.

The urgency of the vision expresses Jesus' reaction to the corruption of the Gospel, and the difficulties faced by his true disciples. It introduces an important section of Revelation where the development and dangers of false religion are graphically described.

Vision 5 – The Lamb on Mount Zion (14:1-20)

Jesus and the saints stand on Mount Zion, and the saints sing for joy because they have been redeemed from among the rest of mankind.

This vision forms an introduction to the seven last plagues, which occur before Jesus returns to set up the kingdom. Despite the fierceness of the plagues, God will ensure that none of Jesus' true disciples is lost.

Vision 6 – God's judgements (15:1-8)

The saints are still singing. Their song is the Song of Moses and of the Lamb, and they stand on the sea of nations, which has been stilled by the work of Jesus.

The stilling of the nations, and exactly how it will occur is only briefly mentioned in Revelation. It is a work symbolised by seven thunders, which John was told not to describe: *"When the seven thunders uttered their voices, I was about to write; but I heard a voice from heaven saying to me, Seal up the things which the seven thunders uttered, and do not write them"* (Revelation 10:4).

Vision 7 – Marriage of the Lamb (19:1-9)

The saints rejoice because Jesus is finally united with his disciples: *"the marriage of the Lamb has come, and his wife has made herself ready"* (19:7).

Together, Jesus and the saints rule over the nations of the world, teaching them of God's ways and putting down all opposition, so that the kingdom can be handed back to God, and He will be "all in all".

Old Testament background

DANIEL AND ZECHARIAH

REVELATION is different from all the other New Testament books, but it has equivalents in the Old Testament – particularly the prophecies of Daniel and Zechariah. We cannot appreciate what Jesus revealed to the Apostle John without first looking at these. Before his death and resurrection, Jesus explained to his disciples the importance of Daniel's message.

The Olivet Prophecy

"As he sat on the Mount of Olives, the disciples came to him privately, saying, 'Tell us, when will these things be? And what will be the sign of your coming, and of the end of the age?'" (Matthew 24:3). Jesus' answer included the following important message: *"When you see the 'abomination of desolation', spoken of by Daniel the prophet, standing in the holy place (whoever reads, let him understand) …"* (verse 15).

We must therefore read, and try to understand Daniel's message. Daniel lived 600 years before the time of Christ. God's nation had been taken captive by the Babylonians, and His people were under the domination of the greatest empire of those times.

When everything seemed utterly hopeless, and God's plan to establish His worldwide kingdom of glory appeared to have failed, God revealed to Daniel what would happen between Daniel's days and the time when His glory will fill the earth.

From Babylon to Rome

We can quickly see the similarity between Daniel and the Apostle John. Daniel lived when Babylon was the ruling power in the earth. In John's day, Babylon's power was only a faint memory, and the Romans dominated the countries of Europe and the Middle East.

Roman soldiers crucified Jesus, and forty years later they destroyed Jerusalem and its great temple. The Jewish people fled and were dispersed into all countries of the world. Once again, it seemed as if God's purpose had failed.

As Daniel was a captive in Babylon, so the Apostle John was a prisoner of Rome on the island of Patmos. The message John received from the Lord Jesus expanded the information revealed to Daniel seven hundred years earlier. He was not told about the Babylonians, nor about the Medes and Persians or the Greeks whose empires succeeded Babylon's. The message to John started in his own day – in the time of the Romans.

Daniel and Revelation

When we look at the two books, there are many similarities. Here are some examples:

- An angel helped Daniel understand the information he was given, and Jesus' angel passed on God's message to John in Revelation.
- Daniel was told that *"The message* (he received) *was true, but the appointed time was long"* (Daniel 10:1). The information given to John explained events that started in his own day and continued through to the return of Christ and the establishment of the kingdom.
- Daniel was a *"man greatly beloved"* (Daniel 10:11), and John was the *"disciple whom Jesus loved"* (John 20:2).
- At the end of the prophecy, Daniel was told to *"shut up the words, and* **seal the book** *until the time of the end"* (Daniel 12:4). At the beginning of Revelation, John was shown *"in the right hand of him who sat on the throne a scroll written inside and on the back,* **sealed with seven seals***"* (Revelation 5:1).

We are obviously expected to see Daniel's prophecy as an introduction to Revelation, and it will help our understanding and appreciation of Jesus' final message if we are reasonably familiar with the following sections of Daniel's prophecy:

- Nebuchadnezzar's dream of the metallic image representing the kingdom of men (Daniel 2).
- Daniel's visions:
  of the four beasts (chapter 7);
  of the Ram and He-Goat (chapter 8);
  of the One Man (chapter 10);
  of the kings of North and South (chapter 11).

The development in Daniel of God's message about the kingdom of men can be seen in the illustration on the opposite page.

Zechariah

But Daniel is not the only Old Testament writer to prophesy about a scroll written on both sides. Ezekiel saw a scroll containing *"lamentations and mourning and woe"* (Ezekiel 2:10), and Zechariah saw a *"flying scroll"* written on *"this side"* and on *"that side"* (Zechariah 5:2,3). He also saw four coloured horses: red, black, white and dappled, like the horses that were unleashed when the Apostle John saw the seven-sealed scroll being unsealed (6:2,3, cp. Revelation 6:2,4,5,8).

Zechariah prophesied to the captives returning from exile in Babylon. He spoke of the restoration of true worship after the idolatry they experienced in Babylon, and he looked forward to the coming of *"the man whose name is the* B<small>RANCH</small>*! From his place he shall branch out, and he shall build the temple of the* L<small>ORD</small>*"* (Zechariah 6:12). This was a prophecy about Jesus that is still to be fulfilled.

Tip

As you read Revelation try to note the references to passages in the Old Testament, and to the teaching of Jesus in the Gospels.

You could mark these to see how their original use helps to explain the message in Revelation.

OLD TESTAMENT BACKGROUND

Development of symbols in Daniel's prophecy

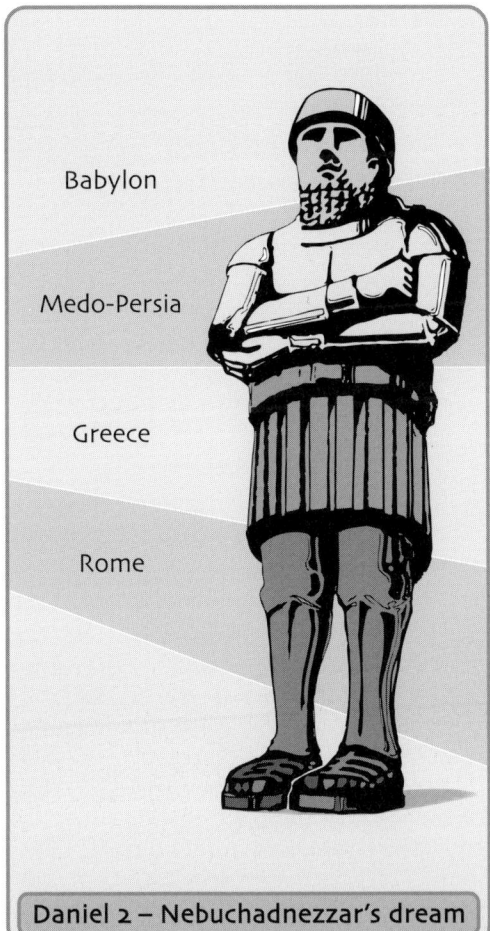

Babylon
Medo-Persia
Greece
Rome

Daniel 2 – Nebuchadnezzar's dream

Babylonian lion
Medo-Persian bear
Grecian Leopard – four wings and heads
Roman beast incorporates ten nations
Holy Roman Empire

Daniel 7 – Daniel's dream

Medo-Persian ram
Grecian goat led by Alexander
Greece under Alexander's successors
Rome
Eastern Roman Empire

Daniel 8 – Daniel's vision

Some of the details of Zechariah's visions therefore reappear in Revelation, and it is helpful to understand something of Zechariah's prophecy to put the message of Revelation in its proper context.

Zechariah also saw a vision of a woman called *"wickedness"* being carried from Jerusalem to a house built for her in the land of Shinar (5:5-11). Shinar was the site of ancient Babylon (Genesis 10:10), and Zechariah's prophecy explained how a false religious system would develop with a Babylonian-like character. Since its earliest times, Babylon has always resisted the truth of God's word.

Other references

References and allusions in Revelation to Old Testament passages are not confined to Daniel and Zechariah. Almost every line in the book is based upon material that was already well known to the book's first readers.

There are references, for example, to the laws and practices of the nation of Israel; some scenes occur in a temple, with incense censers and other items associated with temple worship. Sacrifices are mentioned, and feasts – part of the national life of Israel in Old Testament times.

One of the most significant allusions is to the cherubim that were associated with the tree of life in Eden (Genesis 3:24), and subsequently with the tabernacle and temple in Israel. Cherubim were angelic beings closely associated with God's plan of salvation, and were represented symbolically covering the mercy seat and the ark of the covenant in the tabernacle. Illustrations of cherubim were the only decoration in the tabernacle, and they were depicted with four faces: a lion, ox, man and eagle.

Cherubim appeared in a vision seen by the prophet Ezekiel, who was concerned that God's glory had departed from Jerusalem and the temple. In common with the other prophets, he was concerned lest true worship should be overcome by false worship.

Ezekiel, Daniel and Zechariah naturally asked about the outcome of the revelations they received. Daniel said, *"My lord, what shall be the end of these things?"* (Daniel 12:8). The answer he received leads us straight into the book of Revelation: *"Blessed is he who waits"* (verse 12).

Seven blessings

For Revelation is a book of blessing. Appropriately, there are seven of them.

1 – The Blessing of the Message:

"Blessed is he who reads and those who hear the words of this prophecy, and keep those things which are written in it; for the time is near." (Revelation 1:3)

2 – The Blessing of the Hope:

"Blessed are the dead who die in the Lord from now on … that they may rest from their labours, and their works follow them." (14:13)

3 – The Blessing of Watching:

"Behold, I am coming as a thief. Blessed is he who watches, and keeps his garments, lest he walk naked and they see his shame." (16:15)

4 – The Blessing of the Call:

"Blessed are those who are called to the marriage supper of the Lamb!" (19:9)

5 – The Blessing of Immortality:

"Blessed and holy is he who has part in the first resurrection. Over such the second death has no power, but they shall be priests of God and of Christ, and shall reign with him a thousand years." (20:6)

6 – The Blessing of Obedience:

"Behold, I am coming quickly! Blessed is he who keeps the words of the prophecy of this book." (22:7)

7 – The Blessing of the Kingdom:

"Blessed are those who do his commandments, that they may have the right to the tree of life, and may enter through the gates into the city." (22:14)

The last blessing in Revelation mentions God's faithful people entering into *"the city"*. The book deals with two cities: one is the city of God, the other is the city of man. Because of the connection with Daniel and other Old Testament passages, the city of man is called Babylon. God's city is called New Jerusalem! The story of these two cities is the subject of the next chapter.

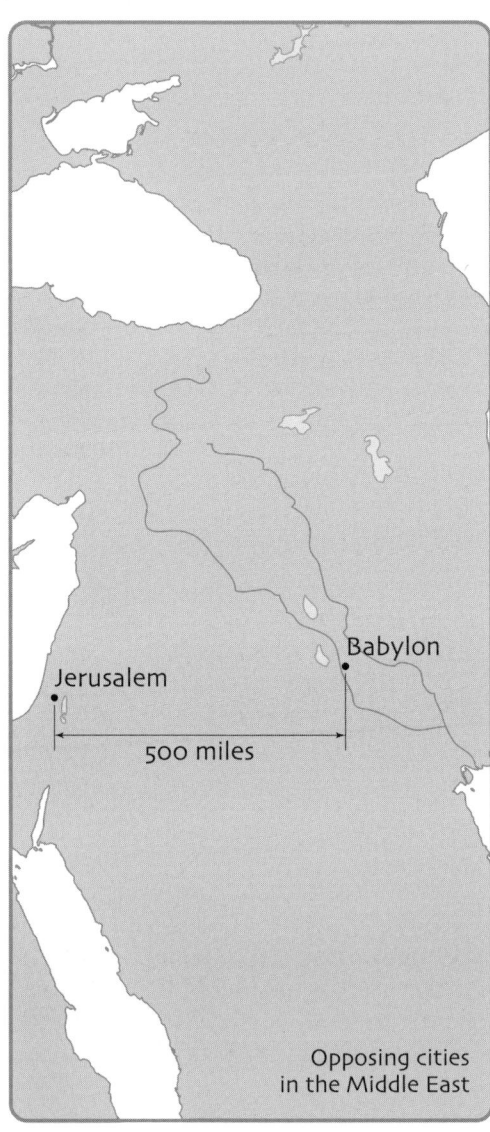

Opposing cities in the Middle East

Tale of two cities

BABYLON AND JERUSALEM

REVELATION is a book of great contrasts. Descriptions of a dreadful Beast are found alongside a vision of a Lamb, who represents the Lord Jesus Christ, *"the Lamb of God who takes away the sin of the world!"* (John 1:29). Similarly, a grotesque and horrible Prostitute confronts a chaste virginal Bride.

In due course, we shall consider the Beast and the Bride. But first of all we must note that the contrasts are particularly noticeable in the case of two opposing cities – Babylon and Jerusalem – standing respectively for the policies and governments of the kingdom of men and the kingdom of God. They are based on real geographical and historical cities, but this information is used symbolically to describe much more than just these two cities.

Desolate and uninhabited

Babylon, for example, no longer existed when John received the Revelation. After its period of glory in the seventh century BC, it gradually decayed. In accordance with God's prophecy through Jeremiah, it became a desolate ruin, and has never recovered its ancient glory (Jeremiah 51:37).

An earlier prophet, Isaiah, writing a hundred years before Babylon's days of glory, said that once the city was destroyed it would never again be populated: *"Babylon, the glory of kingdoms, the beauty of the Chaldeans' pride, will be as when God overthrew Sodom and Gomorrah.* **It will never be inhabited***, nor will it be settled from generation to generation; nor will the Arabian pitch tents there, nor will the shepherds make their sheepfolds there"* (Isaiah 13:19,20).

Babylon in Revelation cannot therefore be the same ancient city; it must be symbolic. But we can learn a lot about the symbolic meaning by looking at the ancient city.

Babel, the great city

First of all, it is very ancient. Babylon is first mentioned in the Bible under its earliest name of Babel, established by one of Noah's great-grandsons: *"Cush begot Nimrod; he began to be a mighty one on the earth. He was a mighty hunter before the* LORD *... And the beginning of his kingdom was* **Babel** *... in the land of Shinar. From that land he went to Assyria and built Nineveh, Rehoboth Ir, Calah, and Resen between Nineveh and Calah (that is the great city)"* (Genesis 10:8-12).

Ancient Babel was famed for its planned high tower, *"whose top is in the heavens"*, intended to prevent its population from being *"scattered abroad over the face of the whole earth"* (11:4). The name signifies "confusion", and refers to the intervention of God in man's grandiose plans, when the universal language was confounded and the city's population dispersed.

What we learn about the original Babylon can be summarised as follows:

- it was devoted to the things of man and not to the things of God;
- it not only opposed God, but provided an alternative focus of worship;
- it was the centre of a kingdom called *"the great city"*;
- it sought to keep people under the domination of its policies.

These factors are carried over into the Babylon of the book of Revelation. It too stands opposed to the things of God, especially in its religious practices. It seeks to dominate its subjects, and is referred to nine times in Revelation as *"that great city"* (Revelation 11:8; 14:8; 16:19; 17:18; 18:10,16,18,19,21).

Where Jesus was crucified

Babylon is only a city in the sense that it has, or desires to have, citizens. But there was one citizen it did not want, and Babylon treats anyone like him as a foreigner. There was no place in Babylon for Jesus Christ, the Lamb of God. According to Revelation, it was *"in the street of* **the great city** *which spiritually is called Sodom and Egypt, where also our Lord was crucified"* (Revelation 11:8).

Spiritually, Babylon is like Sodom and Egypt – so dead to the things of God that it does not recognise true goodness. The followers of Christ cannot be at ease in Babylon, for it is antagonistic to the word of God and the testimony of Jesus.

Revelation uses the figure of the Beast to represent the kingdom of men, and it uses Babylon to emphasise the false religious aspect of that kingdom. The Woman in Revelation was originally a virgin espoused to Jesus, but she became a great harlot when she prostituted her faith. In Revelation 17, we are told that the Woman – the harlot – *"is* **that great city** *which reigns over the kings of the earth"* (Revelation 17:18).

The example of Jericho

The alternative worship provided by Babylon can also be seen in the example of Jericho's destruction in the Old Testament. We have thought about how the Israelites were told to destroy completely everything to do with the city; they must not plunder it to take its spoils. But one man, Achan, did not obey God's command. He took some treasures from the city and buried them under his tent. One item he took was *"a beautiful* **Babylonian** *garment"* (Joshua 7:21). It was "Babylonian" because the city of Jericho, like Babel of old, worshipped

An early 20th century engraving of The Hanging Gardens of Babylon

The old city of Jerusalem today as viewed from the Mount of Olives.

other gods, and refused to submit to the true God of Israel.

Babylon destroyed

The destiny of Babylon's symbolic successor is therefore to be the same as it was for the ancient city of that name, and the same as Jericho's. It will be totally destroyed, because it is a centre of idolatry and uncleanness:

"Babylon the great is fallen, is fallen, and has become a dwelling place of demons, a prison for every foul spirit, and a cage for every unclean and hated bird! ... For her sins have reached to heaven, and God has remembered her iniquities ... she will be utterly burned with fire, for strong is the Lord God who judges her" (Revelation 18:2-8, cp. Jeremiah 51:37).

The city of my God

If Babylon in Revelation describes the false religion of the kingdom of men, what does Jerusalem symbolise? Its position is completely different. Where Babylon was wholly opposed to the things of God, Jerusalem in Revelation upholds everything to do with God and His purpose. Jesus, in his letter to believers at Philadelphia, wrote about *"the city of my God, the New Jerusalem"* (Revelation 3:12). The name of this city is to be inscribed on faithful believers, just as the name of the Beast is marked on the hand or forehead of its subjects (13:16,17).

To bear someone's name is a sign of close association. Naturally speaking, children bear their father's name, and a wife bears her husband's name. To bear the name of the Beast is to become identified with the Beast's intentions. To bear the name of "the city of God" identifies a person with God's purpose.

> *"Great is the Lord, and greatly to be praised In the city of our God, in his holy mountain. Beautiful in elevation, the joy of the whole earth, is Mount Zion on the sides of the north, the city of the great King. God is in her palaces; he is known as her refuge."*
> (Psalm 48:1-3)

If Babylon represents the policies, organisation and government of the false religion that shapes and directs the kingdom of men, then Jerusalem symbolises the policies and organisation of the kingdom of God. These have been determined by God and are related to His eternal purpose in the Lord Jesus Christ. If these policies are to form the basis of government when Jesus returns, they have to be expressed in those who are to govern with Jesus.

At the end of Revelation, therefore, John saw the kingdom of men being replaced: *"I saw a new heaven and a new earth, for the first heaven and the first earth had passed away"* (Revelation 21:1). This new order is described as *"**the great city**, the holy Jerusalem, descending out of heaven from God ... prepared as a bride adorned for her husband"* (Revelation 21:10, 2).

Here again is a great contrast. *"That great city Babylon"* was depicted as a great harlot. *"New Jerusalem"*, the city of God is a Bride, a chaste virgin: *"Its gates shall not be shut at all by day (there shall be no night there). And they shall bring the glory and the honour of the nations into it. But there shall by no means enter it anything that defiles, or causes an abomination or a lie, but only those who are written in the Lamb's book of life"* (verses 25-27).

These two opposing forces are so important to the theme of Revelation that other symbols are also used to reinforce the message. Babylon is always associated with the Beast, and Jerusalem with the Bride, so we shall now consider how these two symbols are developed.

The development of the Beast

GOD'S VIEW OF MAN'S KINGDOM

THERE are two specific Old Testament accounts that introduce the Beast of Revelation. One is in Genesis, the other in Daniel's prophecy.

The Devil and Satan

In Genesis 3, there is the account of Adam and Eve's temptation, and the message of the serpent who questioned the truth of God's command. After their disobedience, Adam and Eve were told of the enmity that would exist between them and the serpent, and between their descendants and the serpent's (Genesis 3:15).

The serpent is therefore used in Revelation and elsewhere in the Bible to describe those who question and deny God's word. In Revelation 12, for example, the Dragon is described as *"that serpent of old, called the Devil and Satan, who deceives the whole world"* (verse 9).

The Dragon is thus a "Devil" – *diabolos* or 'false accuser' – who opposes and falsely accuses the servants of God. It is also "Satan", the Adversary, because it always adopts a position contrary to the ways of God.

The King's dream

The second Old Testament link to the Beast in Revelation is in one of the best known parts of the book of Daniel – Nebuchadnezzar's dream about the kingdom of men. Even though the king could not remember his dream, Daniel through the power of God was able to tell him both what he dreamed, and what the dream meant.

In his dream the king saw a great metallic image in human form. Daniel told Nebuchadnezzar that the image showed the king himself, and then the empires that would succeed his empire of Babylon:

Gold head	Babylon
Silver chest & arms	Medes & Persians
Brass belly & thighs	Greece
Iron legs	Rome

No single kingdom replaced Rome. The image's feet were partly iron and partly clay, representing the situation in the earth immediately before the kingdom of God is established.

As king Nebuchadnezzar watched, the image was crushed to powder by a stone cut out of a mountain without man's help. This stone became a great mountain and filled the whole earth, showing that eventually the kingdom of men will be destroyed and replaced by God's kingdom, which will last forever.

Daniel's dream

Fifty years after the king's dream, when Daniel was an old man, the prophet himself had a dream. He saw four beasts rising out of the sea of nations: a winged lion representing Babylon; a bear representing Medo-Persia; a four-headed and four-winged leopard representing Greece; and a dreadful fourth beast with ten horns (Daniel 7:1-7). Of all the beasts he saw, Daniel wanted to learn more about the fourth beast (verse 19).

Daniel's dream confirms what we have concluded from Nebuchadnezzar's – there are only four empires. Only four kingdoms are mentioned in Daniel 2, and the conditions represented by the feet and toes of iron and clay are just a development of the fourth kingdom. This is especially clear in chapter 7 where Daniel's dream is recorded. In both cases, the fourth kingdom lasts right up until the return of Christ to the earth: *"In the days of these kings the God of heaven will set up a kingdom which shall never be destroyed"* (Daniel 2:44, cp. 7:9-14).

Daniel was also shown that some elements of the earlier kingdoms were present in the fourth beast: it had brass claws, for example (7:19), revealing the presence of certain Greek characteristics.

When John received the Revelation, three of the four kingdoms had passed into history: the Babylonians, Persians and Greeks. He lived when the iron power of Rome ruled the world. If our understanding of Daniel is correct, we should expect to find described in Revelation a power like the legs and feet of the image Nebuchadnezzar saw, and like the fourth beast of Daniel's dream:

- antagonistic to God and His people;
- incorporating features of all the previous kingdoms, and
- eventually developing into a condition where the kingdom's power is mixed throughout all peoples without its essential strength being diminished.

This expectation is realised in the vision of the Beast in Revelation.

The Red Dragon

The Beast is first described fully in Revelation 12 as, *"a great, fiery red dragon having seven heads and ten horns, and seven diadems on his heads"* (verse 3). (There is an earlier reference to *"the beast that ascends out of the bottomless pit"*, in 11:7, but none of its special features are described there.)

This clearly has something to do with Daniel's beasts, for his fourth beast also had ten horns. But if you add the heads on all the beasts he saw, they total seven!

Lion + Bear + Leopard + 4th Beast
 (1) + (1) +   (4)   +   (1)   = 7

This Beast must therefore represent the kingdom of men in totality. Note that it is always called in Daniel a "kingdom"

THE DEVELOPMENT OF THE BEAST

The Dragon in the midst of the waters

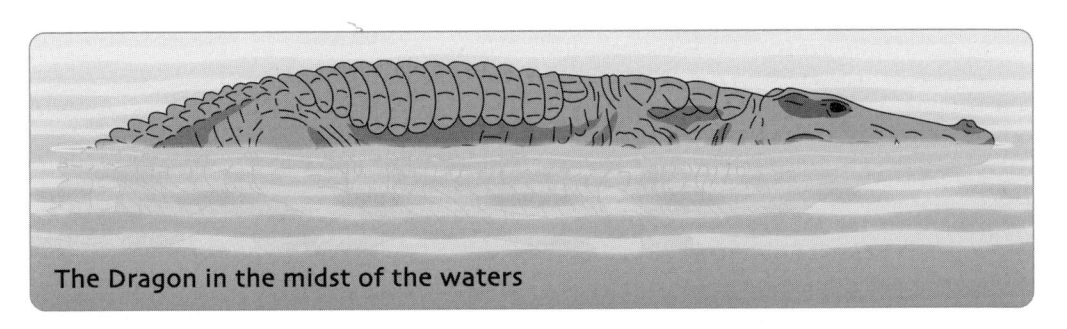

(singular), and never "kingdoms" (plural). This helps to explain why there are various beasts in Revelation, but they are all just aspects of the one fearful Beast Daniel saw *"in the night visions"*.

In the Bible, a dragon always represents an enemy of God's people. Egypt, where the children of Israel were first held captive, was described by Ezekiel as a dragon ready to devour: *"Thus says the Lord GOD: "Behold, I am against you, O Pharaoh king of Egypt, **O great dragon** who lies in the midst of his rivers"* (Ezekiel 29:3). Babylon was also likened by Jeremiah to a dragon who had swallowed him up: *"Nebuchadnezzar the king of Babylon has devoured me, he has crushed me; he has made me an empty vessel, he has swallowed me up **like a dragon**; he has filled his stomach with my delicacies, he has spit me out"* (Jeremiah 51:34).

This caused the prophet to say that the ancient city was ready for destruction. It had acted like a dragon, and was only fit for habitation by dragons: *"Babylon shall become a heap, a dwelling place for dragons, an astonishment and a hissing, without an inhabitant"* (verse 37).

When John received the book of Revelation, Egypt and Babylon were no more. The great enemy of God's people was the Roman power. It too was an ungodly power and tried to destroy all who worshipped the true God.

The Beast of the Sea

The next time we meet the Beast in Revelation, he rises from the Sea, just as Daniel saw in his vision. *"I stood on the sand of the sea. And I saw a beast rising up out of the sea* (cp. Daniel 7:3), *having seven heads and ten horns, and on his horns ten crowns, and on his heads a blasphemous name. Now the beast which I saw was like a leopard, his feet were like the feet of a bear, and his mouth like the mouth of a lion. The dragon gave him his power, his throne, and great authority"* (Revelation 13:1,2)

Here is the same Beast in a new guise. He still has seven heads and ten horns, and power has passed to him from the Dragon. As we learned from Daniel, the Beast has characteristics of all the former kingdoms: he was like a leopard (Greece), with feet like a bear (Medo-Persia), and he spoke like a lion (Babylon).

A mouth speaking great things

All the earth (i.e., the people living in the territories where the Gospel was preached) had worshipped the Dragon; now they worshipped the Beast from the Sea (13:4). As a final confirmation that this account expands the vision of Daniel's fourth beast, we are told that *"he was given a mouth speaking great things"* (verse 5, cp. Daniel 7:8).

In descriptions of the Beast, a lot of attention is paid to the mouth and to what it says. The mouth was like *"the mouth of a lion"*; in other words, it was Babylonian. Throughout the Bible, as we have seen, Babylon is associated with false religion, so the mouth is not only ungodly, as we would expect of a Beast's mouth, it is also blasphemous. The *"great things"* which it speaks are antagonistic to God and His ways, because the Beast claims to be divine.

A head with a deadly wound

There was something special about this Beast's heads. One of them had received a deadly wound, but it had healed. In prophetical symbols, a Beast's head describes its form of government (see panel alongside). This Beast symbolised the revival of a former style of rulership. More information about this development is given in the next vision of the Beast.

The Beast of the Earth

The vision of the Beast of the Sea is followed by one of the Beast of the Earth. This Beast speaks like a dragon (13:11), showing that it is another development of the same fourth kingdom. But it did not have seven heads and ten horns. It had just one head, and two horns – like a lamb.

A Lamb appears elsewhere in Revelation, and always symbolises the Lord Jesus Christ. We should note, however, that this Beast was not really a lamb. It was *"like a lamb"*, but it spoke *"as a dragon"*. Jesus warned his disciples to *"beware of false prophets, who come to you in sheep's clothing, but inwardly they are ravenous wolves"* (Matthew 7:15).

This Beast pretended to be associated with the Lamb, but was really in the direct line of the Dragon. It was a dragon in sheep's clothing promoting a false religion claiming to be Christian.

The Beast's single head, where previously there were seven, indicates that a formerly divided situation has been replaced by a single uniting power. But as there were two horns, this power gave its authority to two rulers. We shall learn in a later section how these were a political and a religious ruler working together.

The Image and the False Prophet

This Beast acted just as Babylon's king Nebuchadnezzar acted centuries before. After Daniel told Nebuchadnezzar about his dream, the king made his own metallic image. It was not made of four metals, but only of one – Gold, the metal representing Babylon and its emperor. Having made it, the king commanded that the image should be worshipped by everyone on pain of death (Daniel 3:6).

The Beast of the Earth was the same: *"He was granted power to give breath to **the image** of the beast, that the image of*

Heads, Horns and Crowns

➤ **HEADS:** Naturally speaking, the head is the centre of control for the whole body, so in symbol the head refers to the controlling power or the government. For example, the emperor Nebuchadnezzar was the *"head of gold"*. Multiple heads (as on the 4-headed Grecian leopard) suggest different forms of government, or different rulers within the same overall kingdom.

➤ **HORNS:** Horns always relate to strength and power wielded by a king or head of state (see 1 Samuel 2:10; Daniel 8:20,21). Multiple horns represent multiple or successive kings.

➤ **CROWNS:** Crowns indicate rulership, and are used to explain the stage of history revealed by the vision. In Revelation 12:3, the Beast's *heads* are crowned; in 13:1, the crowns are on the *horns*, showing that it is a later development.

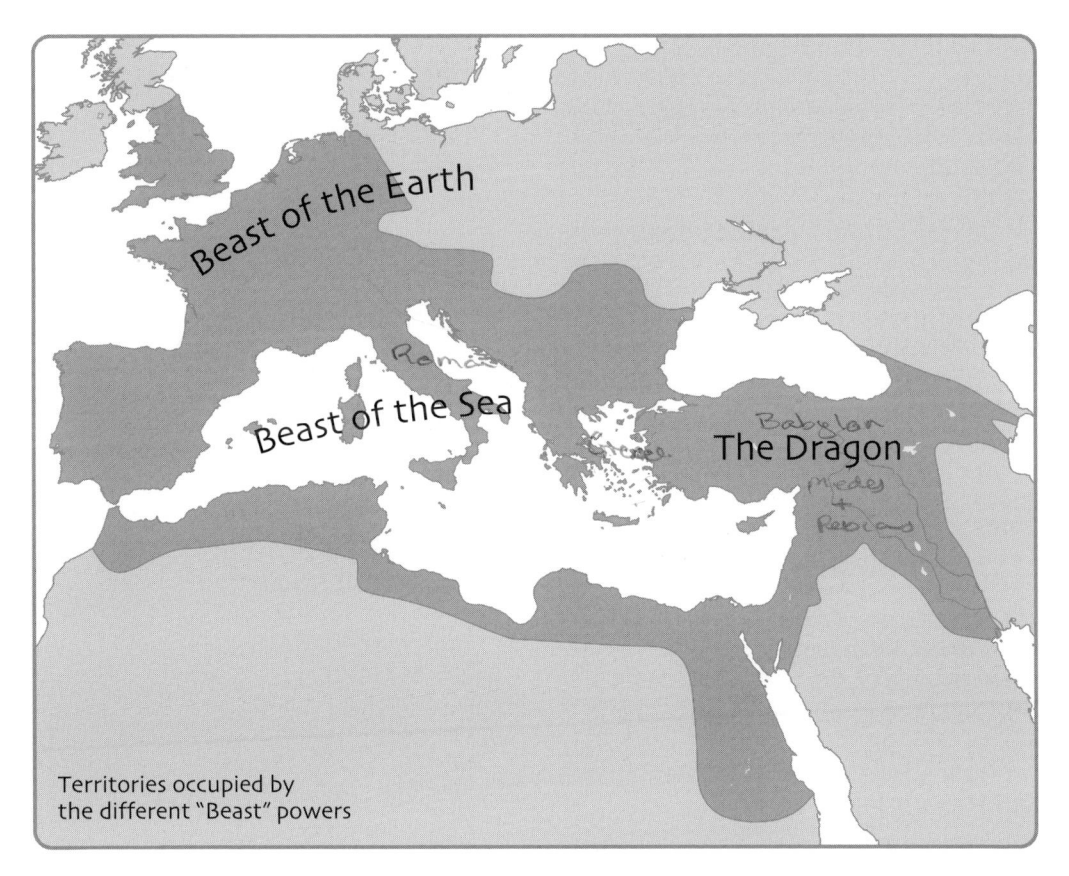

THE DEVELOPMENT OF THE BEAST

Territories occupied by the different "Beast" powers

mouth) are vitally important to the Beast's power over people's lives.

Because it speaks deceitfully, the image of the Beast is later referred to as *"the **false prophet**"* (16:13). This is not surprising, for Jesus warned his disciples that such deceivers would arise (Matthew 7:15; 24:11,24); and the apostles too warned of this development (Acts 20:29; 2 Peter 2:1; 1 John 4:1).

Sea and Earth

Why did one Beast arise from the Sea, and the other from the Earth? This question is even more difficult when we realise that in Revelation both Sea and Earth represent peoples and nations, as we have already discovered (page 12).

Obviously, the information is given to us so that we can distinguish between two sets of people: one that can be termed *"the Sea"*, and the other *"the Earth"*.

There is no doubt that the Beast in John's day was the scarlet coloured Dragon (the pagan Roman Empire). But this Empire did not have fixed boundaries: it comprised various different parts. First of all, it divided into two – an Eastern and Western part, as indicated by the two legs of the image in Nebuchadnezzar's dream. The Dragon – originally the whole pagan Roman Empire – was displaced by the newly emerging 'Christian' government, and was left in control of the Eastern half.

Various other changes occurred over the centuries. The Western part also divided

the beast should both speak and cause as many as would not worship the image of the beast to be killed" (Revelation 13:15).

The image and mouth of the Beast are obviously important, relating it closely to Babylon. The Beast is a master of public relations: what is displayed outwardly (the image) and what is heard publicly (the

31

into two sections: the areas bordering the Mediterranean Sea, and the continental land mass of Europe. How fitting to describe one of these as the Earth (Continental Europe), and the other as the Sea (Mediterranean lands). These divisions are shown on the accompanying map depicting the Roman Empire in the 5th century AD. These two parts of the Western section of the Empire were ruled by the Beast of the Sea and the Beast of the Earth.

A scarlet coloured Beast

Finally, in Revelation 17, the last phase of the Beast's development is described: *"I saw a woman sitting on a scarlet beast which was full of names of blasphemy, having seven heads and ten horns ... And on her forehead a name was written: MYSTERY, BABYLON THE GREAT, THE MOTHER OF HARLOTS AND OF THE ABOMINATIONS OF THE EARTH"* (verses 3-5).

The Woman is discussed in more detail in the next chapter. All we need to know at this stage is that under her control, the Beast opposes the Lord Jesus when he returns to earth to set up God's kingdom.

A lake of fire

The Woman encourages the Beast to make war with the Lamb – the Lord Jesus Christ – and with his faithful followers (Revelation 17:12-14). Finding itself unable to win the battle, the Beast turns on the Woman and destroys her, before finally being overpowered by Jesus himself: *"The beast was captured, and with him the false prophet ... these two were cast alive into the lake of fire burning with brimstone"* (19:20). This is also how the wicked cities of Sodom and Gomorrah were destroyed (see Genesis 19:24).

But the Dragon is not to be destroyed at the same time. In Revelation 20:1-3, we are told that when Jesus returns the Dragon is cast into the bottomless pit from where it first emerged (cp. 11:7). The Dragon still has work to do. At the end of a thousand years – the Millennium when Jesus and his faithful followers bring the world into subjection to the rule of God – the Dragon is allowed to rebel for one last and final time.

This final rebellion ends when God destroys the Dragon as decisively as the Beast and False Prophet were destroyed: *"The devil, who deceived them, was cast into the lake of fire and brimstone where the beast and the false prophet are"* (Revelation 20:10).

Only when the Beast is completely destroyed will God's power be seen in all the earth. The Beast's career will then finally be ended.

DCLXVI

What does this inscription mean? Turn to page 71 to find out.

Corrupt religion

BELIEVERS FACING GREATER TRIBULATION

THE Beast shows its most beastly characteristics when it confronts the followers of the Lord Jesus Christ. This is the same great contrast as we saw in the opposition of the two cities Babylon and Jerusalem.

As we have seen, the Beast in its last phase gives over its power to *"a woman"*. It is significant that a Woman first appears in Revelation at the same time as the Beast is first introduced. In chapter 12 where we first meet the *"great red dragon"*, he stands before a Woman who is about to give birth, intending to devour her child as soon as it is born.

A Woman

Prophetically, a "Woman" represents both men *and* women and how they respond to God's call. In the Book of Proverbs, for example, two women are described, one called Wisdom and one called Folly. "Wisdom" builds her house on sure foundations (Proverbs 9:1; 14:1); "Folly" is pictured as *"a strange woman ... an adulteress"* (6:24-29).

The same contrast occurs in Revelation. "Wisdom" is the chaste Bride, and "Folly" the corrupt Prostitute. Both women originate from the believers who were *"added to the Lord"* through the preaching of the apostles after Jesus' death and resurrection.

The "Woman" in Revelation therefore represents a group of religious believers. If the group is faithful and true, the woman is pure and chaste. If it is corrupt or in error, the woman is unfaithful: she has adulterated her faith. The Prostitute in Revelation 17 describes a religious system claiming to be faithful to Jesus, but corrupt, like ancient Babylon: given over to idolatry, greed, blasphemy, and to the persecution of God's faithful people.

The Beast and the Prostitute meet their end when they rise up against the Lord Jesus when he returns to the earth. The conditions he will find when he comes are ones where the real power behind the throne of the kingdom of men is a false system of Christianity, manipulating events for its own evil purposes.

We have spent some time looking at the career of the Beast and how it comes under the control of a false religious system, but it is much more important to track the development and divine protection of those whom Jesus will recognise as his friends when he returns to the earth, and who as

Many religions are associated with illustrations of women. Ancient Ephesus worshipped Diana (Artemis).

his Bride will comprise faithful believers from all ages.

Jesus' servants

This is the group of people for whom the book of Revelation is primarily intended. They are *"his – i.e., Jesus' – servants"* (Revelation 1:1). They are always evident in the visions of the kingdom:

- as elders;
- as living creatures reflecting the divine qualities of the *"living God"* whom they serve;
- as a great multitude clothed in white garments;
- as 144,000 bearing God's Name on their foreheads;
- and finally as a Bride prepared to meet her husband.

The great variety of ways this group of faithful servants is described shows how important they are in the scheme of the book as a whole. We are intended to identify with them at each stage if we are going to be counted among their number when Jesus returns.

Congregations praying

These individuals are not left alone, nor are they expected to be on their own. There are always faithful *groups* of believers. In chapter 1, for example, they are seen in symbol as *lampstands*, because they witness congregationally to the truth of the Gospel in the darkness of the world. John is given an explanation of *"the mystery of … the seven golden lampstands … the seven lampstands which you saw are the seven churches"* (Revelation 1:20).

Nor are these groups of believers inactive. Throughout Revelation they are shown to be constantly praying to God, urging Him to act on their behalf and to hasten His purpose. They are seen in His Temple, as if they are constantly in God's presence. And their prayers are answered. Each new set of divine judgements falling on the kingdom of men is a direct consequence of the believers' prayers.

But all the while their position is under attack. They live in an ungodly world that fails to recognise God's majesty. More seriously, men and women who claim to be followers of Jesus have corrupted the true Gospel. The Lord warned of the dangers of *"false Christs"* and of false Christianity, and Revelation expands this warning to prepare his true followers for the teaching they must endure and overcome.

They must *"wash their robes … in the blood of the Lamb"* (Revelation 7:14), and be clothed in white linen *"for the fine linen is the righteous acts of the saints"* (19:8). All this happens to those who come out of the Great Tribulation; it is a process whereby the faithful are revealed and the unfaithful are exposed for what they really are.

Attacks on the Truth

As a warning to remain faithful, Revelation shows how easily truth becomes tarnished and corrupt when it is contained in frail human hands. There were already problems in John's day when he received the Revelation from Jesus. Faithful believers were being affected by some of their own number who were described as *"Jezebel"*, after Israel's most wicked queen (2:20; cp. 1 Kings 16:31). Jesus said the situation was so bad that their lampstand would be taken away if things did not improve.

The real threat to Jesus' servants arose from persecution. John himself had been imprisoned and exiled by the Romans. This persecution was at its most fierce when false believers united with the political powers. This was nothing new, for the Jewish leaders conspired with Rome to crucify Jesus, and the same pattern has been repeated many times since in the lives of Jesus' followers.

The Woman and her offspring

Revelation shows how quickly believers compromised their position with the political powers. In chapter 12, for example, a Woman who was meant to be a chaste virgin was *"with child"*. Prophetically, she represents a community of believers who compromised the truth and did not remain faithful to Christ. Yet even among these there were some individuals who remained faithful: *"the rest of her offspring, who keep the commandments of God and have the testimony of Jesus Christ"* (12:17). Revelation focuses on this group, and shows how Jesus' faithful disciples will be rewarded when he returns.

Consistently throughout the book we are reminded of *"the patience and the faith of the saints"* (13:10). Whatever befalls them, they must remain true to the things of God if they are to receive the reward of a place in His kingdom.

Circumstances cannot improve so long as Jesus is still absent from the earth. We learn of those *"who had been beheaded for their witness to Jesus and for the word of God, who had not worshipped the beast or his image, and had not received his mark on their foreheads or on their hands"* (20:4).

Prepared as a Bride

The whole process is one of preparation. Out of this time of testing comes eventually the community that Jesus will recognise when he returns. Individual believers are preparing and being prepared for that day in the same way as a bride makes preparations for her wedding. Eventually, the only "Woman" who is left will be the Bride of Christ: *"Let us be glad and rejoice and give him glory, for the marriage of the Lamb has come, and his wife has made herself ready"* (19:7).

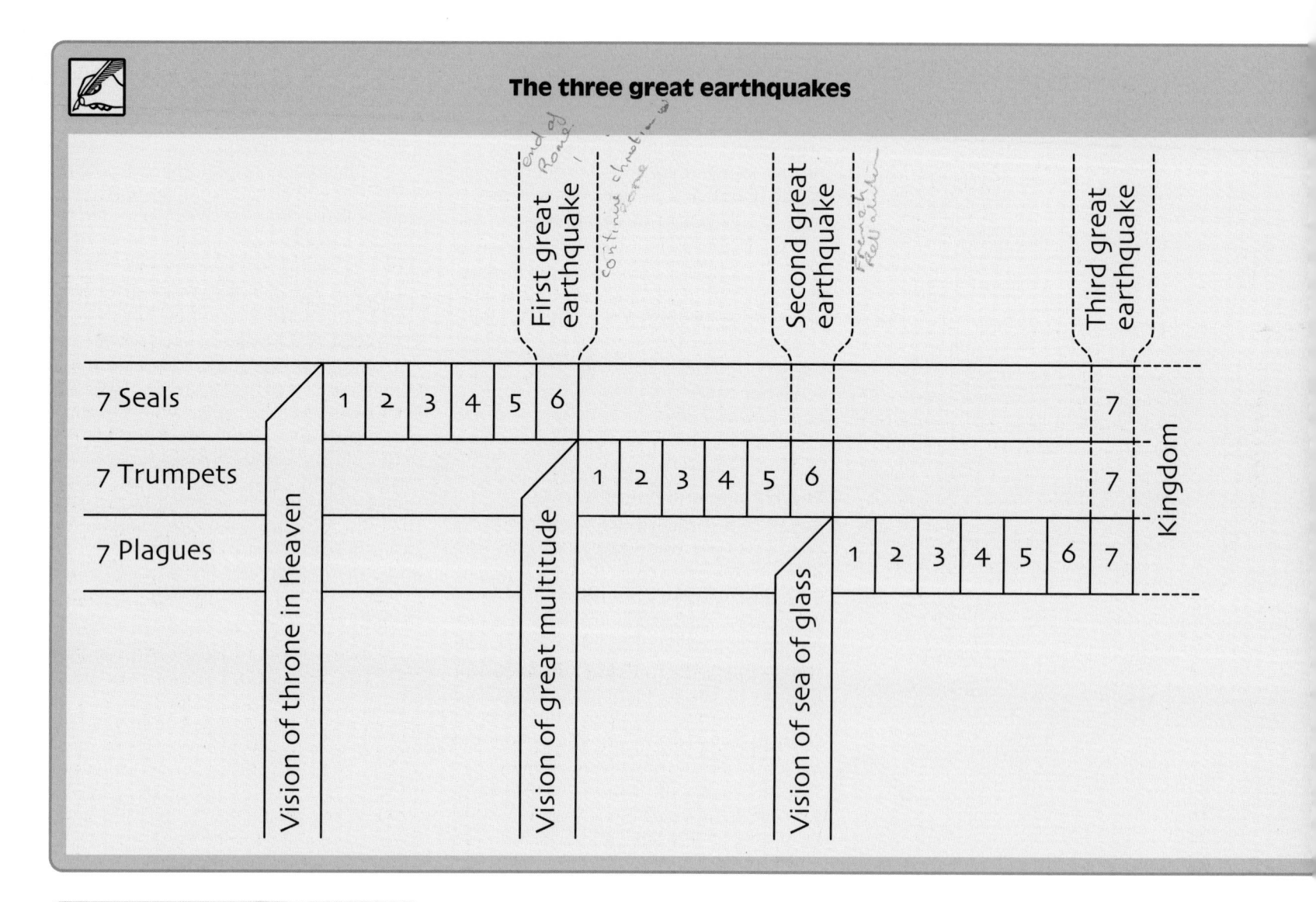

The three great earthquakes

| | First great earthquake | Second great earthquake | Third great earthquake |

Handwritten annotations:
- First great earthquake: "End of Rome", "continue christian zone"
- Second great earthquake: "French Revolution"

Chart structure:

- **7 Seals**: 1, 2, 3, 4, 5, 6 7
- **7 Trumpets**: 1, 2, 3, 4, 5, 6 7
- **7 Plagues**: 1, 2, 3, 4, 5, 6, 7

Vertical labels:
- Vision of throne in heaven
- Vision of great multitude
- Vision of sea of glass
- Kingdom

Three earthquakes

➤ *"I looked when he opened the sixth seal, and behold, there was a great earthquake; and the sun became black as sackcloth of hair, and the moon became like blood."* (Revelation 6:12)

➤ *"In the same hour there was a great earthquake, and a tenth of the city fell. In the earthquake seven thousand people were killed, and the rest were afraid and gave glory to the God of heaven."* (Revelation 11:13)

➤ *"And there were noises and thunderings and lightnings; and there was a great earthquake, such a mighty and great earthquake as had not occurred since men were on the earth."* (Revelation 16:18)

Three great earthquakes

CHANGES IN WORLD RULERSHIP

clue 7

THE last of our seven clues is to watch out for the three *"great earthquakes"* in Revelation. These mark important political changes affecting the lives of God's people at different stages in the development of His purpose. Natural earthquakes are upheavals of the earth's crust. In Bible prophecy, earthquakes affect the people who live on earth by radically changing the conditions under which they live.

Reinforcing the important threefold judgements of seals, trumpets and plagues, one earthquake occurs towards the end of the seals period, one towards the end of the trumpets period, and the third when the seventh plague is finally poured out. This last earthquake is described differently from the other two. It was *"such a mighty and great earthquake as had not occurred since men were on the earth"* (Revelation 16:18).

The kingdom of God is established

As this earthquake occurs right at the end of God's judgements on human government, it marks the transition from the kingdom of men to the kingdom of God, when Jesus returns. The new government to be set up on the earth after the former powers are removed will last for a thousand years. Jesus will be the new ruler, and his faithful disciples will assist him (20:6).

This *"earthquake"* is the one mentioned by the prophet Zechariah when he talks of Jesus returning to the Mount of Olives, from where he ascended into heaven. *"The Mount of Olives shall be split in two, from east to west, making a very large valley … Yes, you shall flee as you fled from the earthquake in the days of Uzziah king of Judah. Thus the LORD my God will come, and all the saints with you"* (Zechariah 14:4,5).

Other prophets mention the same thing. Isaiah, for example, says that men and women will *"go into the holes of the rocks, and into the caves of the earth, from the terror of the LORD and the glory of his majesty, when he arises to shake the earth mightily"* (Isaiah 2:19).

These two prophecies suggest that the political upheaval that will occur when Jesus returns may also be accompanied by a literal (physical) earthquake that will destroy man's structures and make way for the new arrangements in God's kingdom. Jesus himself, speaking of events that would prepare the world for his return said: *"Nation will rise against nation, and kingdom against kingdom. And there will be great earthquakes in various places ..."* (Luke 21:10,11).

If the third *"great earthquake"* describes Jesus' return, what about the two other *"great earthquakes"*? They divide into three sections the time from when John received Revelation to the time of Jesus' return. These three sections are described in Revelation as the seals period, the trumpets period, and the plagues period. The *"great earthquakes"* mark the transition from one period to the next.

Paganism gives way to Christianity

When John was exiled in Patmos, the iron power of Rome held full sway. The Roman Caesar of that day (most probably Domitian, AD81-96) persecuted the followers of Jesus, and ruled over a largely pagan empire. 'Pagans' are people who do not recognise the existence of the one true God, and who worship gods of their own invention.

A government claiming to be Christian replaced this pagan form of rulership. This was such a remarkable and drastic occurrence that *"a great earthquake"* fittingly represents the change. It heralded the start of a new epoch: pagan Rome became 'Christian' Rome in the 4th century AD, but it was not really the Christianity taught by Jesus and the apostles. It was both corrupt and corrupting: a deadly mixture of religion, politics and human greed.

God judged pagan Rome for persecuting Jesus' followers, shown in Revelation when the seven-sealed scroll was gradually unrolled. After the first *"great earthquake"*, more judgements occurred. But these required a different symbol: seven trumpet judgements replaced the seven-sealed scroll, and God judged 'Christian' Rome for corrupting His truth. These judgements came by means of attacks on the Empire from outside its boundaries: by barbarian tribes from the north and by Islamic tribes from the east. They ended with the second *"great earthquake"*.

Revolutions

The rule of Christendom was replaced by earth-shattering events. The long period when power was in the hands of a small minority of kings, princes and religious leaders drastically ended when people began to unite and demand power themselves. The American and French Revolutions in the 18th century AD overthrew the power of church and state, replacing the old hierarchical systems with a new form of government "of the people, by the people, and for the people", as Abraham Lincoln, the American President called it. This period of revolutions is described in Revelation as the second *"great earthquake"* affecting the world where Jesus' followers are living.

Just as natural (literal) earthquakes are often followed by 'aftershocks', the effect of symbolic earthquakes can continue for long periods of time. The revolutionary earthquakes that started in France have affected world politics with almost 250 years of continuous upheavals.

As a result of these cataclysmic changes, another new epoch started, and a new sequence of God's judgements – this time represented by seven plagues. These plagues fell on a divided kingdom, as we know from the feet and toes of the image seen in Nebuchadnezzar's dream, and from information in Revelation. The Dragon, the Beast, and the False Prophet all co-exist. But they are affected by a policy, constantly at work amongst them – a policy as strong as the iron that was first used to symbolise the might and power of Rome. The book of Revelation describes how a strong union between political rulers and corrupt religion controls the affairs of the kingdom of men in the era leading up to the return of the Lord Jesus Christ.

The greatest earthquake of all

It will undoubtedly need a very great earthquake to displace the unholy alliance between political and religious powers that currently dominates every nation on earth. But when it is removed, the way will be clear for God's rule and peace to permeate throughout the world.

Seven introductory letters

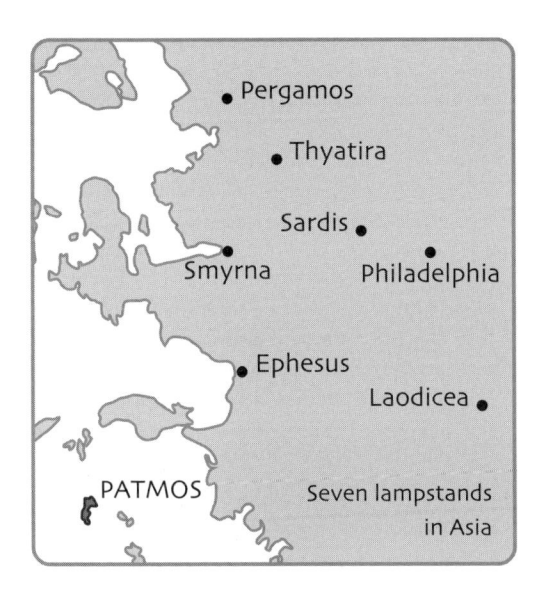

Seven lampstands in Asia (map showing Pergamos, Thyatira, Sardis, Smyrna, Philadelphia, Ephesus, Laodicea, and Patmos)

WITH the benefit of the seven clues we have considered, we now turn to the book and look at its various parts in greater detail. The first main section contains seven letters, and is introduced, as we have discovered, by a vision of the kingdom. The letters are from the Lord Jesus Christ, and are addressed to groups of believers living in the Roman province of Asia at the time when John received the original message in the closing years of the first century AD (see map alongside).

Seven lampstands

These groups of believers are described as *"seven golden lampstands"* (2:1). Jesus taught his disciples to *"Let your light so shine before men, that they may see your good works and glorify your Father in heaven"* (Matthew 5:16). If individual believers are *"lights"*, groups of believers are *"lampstands"*, holding forth the Gospel message in teaching and practice. So we read in Revelation, *"the seven lampstands which you saw are the seven churches"* (1:20).

The seven letters contain a message from Jesus to each of these groups of believers appropriate to their unique circumstances at the time when the letters were written. But the lessons are also appropriate for those who live in later generations. In common with every major section of the book, the letters are introduced by a vision of the kingdom when Jesus will rule over the world with the assistance of his faithful followers. We are expected to see those who received the letters not just as first century believers, but as representing groups of believers in every age – from the time when John was living, right through to the time when Jesus returns to the earth in glory.

The important connections between the letters and the Introductory Vision can be seen from the chart overleaf. From this we can see that the details of the Vision are woven into the fabric of all the letters, showing that the Vision has something to do with the believers who received the messages.

Vision of "One like the Son of Man"

The Vision sets the scene, not just for the letters that follow it, but also for the whole book of Revelation. It is therefore very important to understand it correctly.

John saw in the midst of seven golden lampstands, *"One like the Son of Man"*. It is immediately apparent that this is a symbolic figure: he holds seven stars in his right hand, and has a two-edged sword coming out of his mouth. His feet are like brass, and his voice is like the sound of many waters.

Many of these pieces of information take us to other visions in the Old Testament. Ezekiel's vision of the Cherubim (Ezekiel 1), and especially Daniel's vision of *"a certain man"* (Daniel 10), provide the keys to understand the vision which John saw in Revelation (see comparison below).

The *"One like the Son of Man"* is representative of Jesus united with his faithful followers. It is a vision because it has not yet been seen in reality. Many of Jesus' followers have died, and some people have still to choose to follow him. Only when Jesus returns will *all* his faithful followers be gathered to his side.

In the Vision, there was a *"voice as the sound of many waters"* – i.e., many people praising with "one voice". The feet were of brass: a metal used in the Bible to denote mankind's earthy nature and its tendency to sin. But the brass was *"fine"* or *"burnished"*, showing that a process of refining has taken place, as Jesus' followers who have tried to overcome temptation and devote themselves to his service are made immortal.

Integral with the rest of Revelation

Sometimes, the first three chapters of Revelation are treated as if they are separate from the rest of the book. Either they are passed over quickly so that a lot of attention can be paid to the remaining chapters, or the letters are examined in

One like the Son of Man

"In the midst of the seven lampstands (I saw) One like the Son of Man, clothed with a garment down to the feet and girded about the chest with a golden band. His head and hair were white like wool, as white as snow, and his eyes like a flame of fire; his feet were like fine brass, as if refined in a furnace, and his voice as the sound of many waters; he had in his right hand seven stars, out of his mouth went a sharp two-edged sword, and his countenance was like the sun shining in its strength." (Revelation 1:13-16)

The Cherubim

"Their legs were straight, and the soles of their feet were like the soles of calves' feet. They sparkled like the colour of burnished bronze." (Ezekiel 1:7)

A certain Man

"I lifted my eyes and looked, and behold, a certain man clothed in linen, whose waist was girded with gold of Uphaz! His body was like beryl, his face like the appearance of lightning, his eyes like torches of fire, his arms and feet like burnished bronze in colour, and the sound of his words like the voice of a multitude." (Daniel 10:5,6)

How the promises in the

➤ Will eat of the tree of life in Paradise – *"In the middle of its street, and on either side of the river, was the tree of life, which bore twelve fruits, each tree yielding its fruit every month. The leaves of the tree were for the healing of the nations"* (22:2).

➤ Will not be hurt of the second death – *"Then Death and Hades were cast into the lake of fire. This is the second death"* (20:14).

➤ Will eat of the Hidden Manna (a golden pot of manna was placed in the ark of the covenant, in the heart of the tabernacle, Exodus 16:33, Hebrews 9:4, symbolising God's promise to look after His people for ever) – *"Behold, the tabernacle of God is with men, and he will dwell with them, and they shall be his people"* (21:3).

➤ Will have a white stone with a new name (a white stone was used as a sign of acquittal in Roman courts) – *"Behold, I am coming quickly, and my reward is with me, to give to every one according to his work"* (22:12).

➤ Will have power over the nations to rule with a rod of iron – *"The armies in heaven, clothed in fine linen, white and clean, followed him on white horses. Now out of his mouth goes a

SEVEN INTRODUCTORY LETTERS

7 letters will be fulfilled

sharp sword, that with it he should strike the nations. And he himself will rule them with a rod of iron" (19:14,15).

➤ Will have the Morning Star – *"I, Jesus, have sent my angel to testify to you these things in the churches. I am the Root and the Offspring of David, the Bright and Morning Star"* (22:16).

➤ Will be clothed in white – *"And the armies in heaven, clothed in fine linen, white and clean, followed him on white horses"* (19:14).

➤ Will have a name in the Book of Life – *"And I saw the dead, small and great, standing before God, and books were opened. And another book was opened ... anyone not found written in the book of life was cast into the lake of fire"* (20:12-15).

➤ Will be a pillar in God's Temple, bearing His Name, and the name of New Jerusalem – *"I, John, saw the holy city, New Jerusalem, coming down out of heaven from God, prepared as a bride adorned for her husband."* (21:2).

➤ Will sit with Jesus in his throne – *"And I saw thrones, and they sat on them, and judgment was committed to them ... And they lived and reigned with Christ for a thousand years"* (20:4).

great detail with little reference (if any) to later sections of the book. Both of these approaches miss the important connections between the Introductory Vision and letters, and the later sections of the book with all their details about God's dealings with the powers who persecute His people.

The table alongside, with its details of how the promises in the letters are fulfilled in the final chapters, shows how these connections are deeply embedded in the text of Revelation.

If the letters are an integral part of the book, as we have seen, what is their real purpose? From the details of the Introductory Vision, we learn that believers are to *"grow into a holy temple in the Lord"* (Ephesians 2:21). Once Jesus has returned and called his faithful disciples into the kingdom, they will be united with him forever. Through them and their work, Christ's rule will spread throughout the world.

A perfect man

In order to prepare for that time, believers should try to be like Jesus now, reflecting his characteristics to the best of their ability. A description of this process can be found in Ephesians 4. It started with the work of the apostles, and then, when the scripture record was complete, it was continued by the inspired word of God. This message was given to Jesus' disciples, *"for the equipping of the saints for the work of ministry, for the edifying of the body of Christ, till we all come to the unity of the faith and of the knowledge of the Son of God, to **a perfect man**, to the measure of the stature of the fullness of Christ"* (Ephesians 4:12,13).

The *"Perfect Man"* in this quotation is the Man seen in vision by John and recorded in Revelation 1. This "Man" comprises men and women from every age who have placed their faith and hope in the promises of God, and whose hope will be rewarded by immortality when Jesus returns.

The man of Christ

As Revelation was a message from Jesus for his servants and those who will be his servants, the importance of the Introduction (Revelation chapters 1-3) should now be clear. The whole book is about how the Man of Christ will be developed in an ungodly world. It is about how divine characteristics will be displayed by the true followers of Jesus in their lifetime, despite persecution and oppression; and how eventually these qualities will fill the earth with God's glory. It tells us that God's purpose will be fulfilled, and man's domination of the earth will not last forever. The message gives us confidence that the power of God's word, creating faith in men and women, is greater than all worldly powers.

Redemption through Christ

Jesus is therefore described right at the beginning of the book as the one *"who loved us and washed us* (or, loosed us, RV) *from our sins in his own blood"* (1:5). The basis of redemption is thus established at the outset. The response of individuals to the call of the Gospel, and how God acts on their behalf when they call upon Him for help, is the theme of the book.

The other message of the seven letters is that believers are not left on their own. Primarily, Jesus promises to be with them in every circumstance of life; but they are also encouraged to join together with other believers to become lampstands of truth in a dark world. The contents of the seven letters are therefore both for individual believers to contemplate, and for groups of believers to consider carefully. These groups meeting in different cities are called "churches" in our English translations, but the original word (Greek, *ekklesia*) refers specifically to a group of people who have been called out of general society for a particular purpose. The Acts of the Apostles explains how: *"God at the first visited the Gentiles to take out of them a people for his name"* (Acts 15:14).

Representative ecclesias?

Considering that the stage on which the drama of Revelation is played out is the territory inhabited by believers in Christ, we might expect the seven groups of believers who received individual letters from the Lord Jesus Christ to be spread right across the late first-century Roman Empire. But the seven letters were sent to ecclesias grouped quite closely together in the western part of Asia Minor, within the territory we now know as Turkey. Are they therefore really representative of *all* ecclesias?

The importance of their location is apparent as soon as we look at a map of the Empire. The main route from Rome to the East runs through the centre of Asia Minor, and anyone travelling towards Syria, Palestine or Egypt would pass through most of the cities mentioned in Revelation 2 and 3. Add to this the cosmopolitan nature of the population, and the different characteristics of the seven cities, and any doubt that they are representative of all ecclesias soon disappears.

The central location of the Seven Lampstands

1. Ephesus

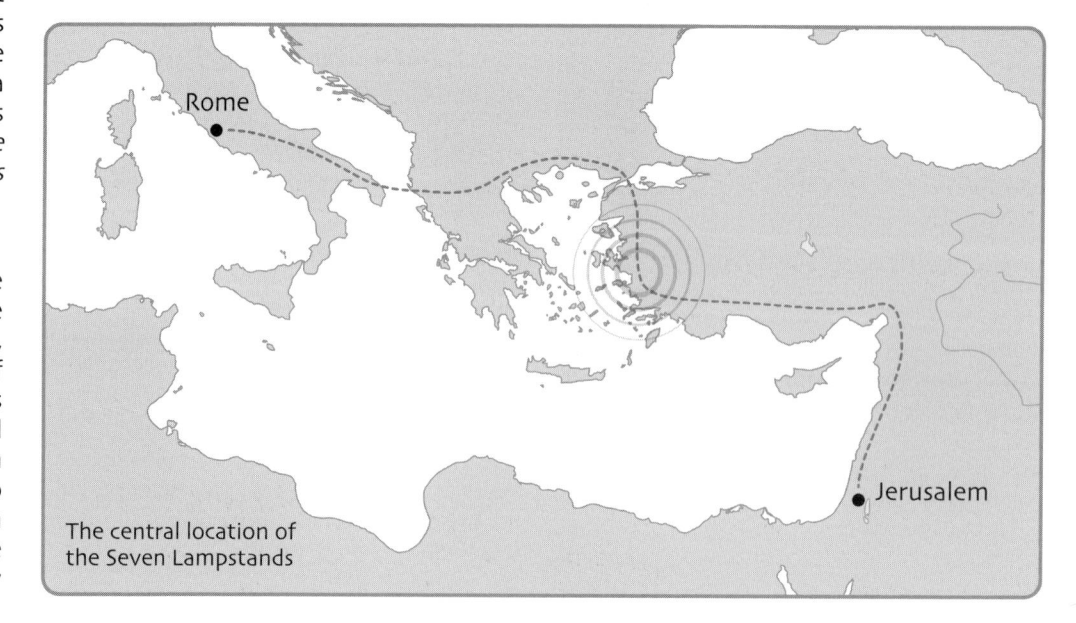

Was the leading city in the province of Asia, and the provincial capital. It was also the most prominent ecclesia in the locality, and is mentioned frequently in the New Testament. The Apostle John had settled in Ephesus, and it was from here that he was exiled to Patmos. Ephesian society was centred on worship of the goddess Artemis, or Diana, and the Apostle Paul came into conflict with her worshippers during his stay in the city. Jesus' letter to Ephesus mentions the problem caused by the Nicolaitans, believed to be a group that was tolerant of sexual immorality, and this would also be associated with the city's idolatry. In every way, life in Ephesus was like a microcosm of the conflict depicted in Revelation between true believers in Christ and the beast and its worshippers.

2. Smyrna

Was situated about 35 miles north of Ephesus, and was famed for its wealth and splendour. It was the first city outside Rome to build a temple to the goddess Roma, and among the first to introduce emperor-worship. By allowing the imperial subjects to continue worshipping their historical deities, and by introducing emperor worship as well, Rome managed to quell revolt and strengthen the links between conquered territories and Rome. Disloyalty to the emperor, not regarding him as "lord over all", was severely punished. Among the other gods worshipped in Smyrna was the god of wine, Dionysius or Bacchus, and this contributed to corruption and immorality in the city.

3. Pergamum

Was another 60 miles north and a royal city. It had an illustrious library, rivalling the one in Alexandria, and was the birthplace of parchment, invented when Egypt banned the export of papyrus. It was full of idols' temples, with one dedicated to Aesculapius the god of healing. Pergamum was renowned as a health centre in the Empire, but like Ephesus it tolerated the Nicolaitans.

4. Thyatira

Was a city that grew up for commercial reasons. It was famed as the centre of the dyeing trade, and its speciality was purple dye produced from the root of the madder plant (Lydia, in Acts 16, was from Thyatira and a *"seller of purple"*, verse 14). With other associated trades also centred in the city, the guilds or associations wielded much influence among the people and made life hard for any who refused conscientiously to be involved. The ecclesia in Thyatira also suffered the malign influence of a prominent sister who did not stand aside from the immorality that was rife in the city; she also encouraged others to abandon the Christian way of life.

5. Sardis

Was well situated for defence, and was formerly capital of the kingdom of Lydia. It was the centre for trade in wool and woollen fabrics, and dyeing was invented in Sardis, though later it became more associated with Thyatira. The fabulously wealthy Lydian king, Croesus, made Sardis his capital, leading to a reputation for the Sardians of loose-living and unbridled luxury. Relying on its famed impregnability, Sardis fell prey to resourceful attackers, such as Cyrus the Mede who took the city *"like a thief in the night"* (cp. Revelation 3:3).

6. Philadelphia

Was a comparatively modern city, established in the second century BC in a volcanic and earthquake-prone region. The soil was fertile and used for vineyards, and the hot springs attracted the weak and infirm to bathe there.

7. Laodicea

Was about 100 miles along the great Eastern trade route from Ephesus. Before it was incorporated in the Roman Empire it was vulnerable to attack because of its reliance on a water supply brought by aqueduct from springs several miles away. The springs were hot springs, but the aqueduct meant that Laodicea's water was always lukewarm (cp. Revelation 3:15). The city flourished under Roman rule, becoming a centre for banking and finance. Its wealth is testified by the fact that it did not seek imperial assistance towards rebuilding after an earthquake in AD60. The city was rich, and had need of nothing (cp. Revelation 3:17).

The message for us

Each letter contains the same major features (see chart on pages 44, 45):

- an assessment by Jesus of their works;
- any failings he perceives;
- a warning, and
- a promise for all who "overcome".

As we read them, we should think of our own position. What would Jesus say about us? How would he assess the lives we lead? What warning would he give us? And what hope lies before us?

Ecclesia	Ephesus	Smyrna	Pergamum	Thyatira
Extract from opening vision	"These things says he who holds the seven stars in his right hand, who walks in the midst of the seven golden lampstands:"	"These things says the First and the Last, who was dead, and came to life:"	"These things says He who has the sharp two-edged sword:"	"These things says the Son of God, who has eyes like a flame of fire, and his feet like fine brass:"
Jesus' assessment	"I know your works, your labour, your patience, and that you cannot bear those who are evil. And you have tested those who say they are apostles and are not, and have found them liars; and you have persevered and have patience, and have laboured for my name's sake and have not become weary."	"I know your works, tribulation, and poverty (but you are rich); and I know the blasphemy of those who say they are Jews and are not, but are a synagogue of Satan. Do not fear any of those things which you are about to suffer. Indeed, the devil is about to throw some of you into prison, that you may be tested, and you will have tribulation ten days. Be faithful until death, and I will give you the crown of life."	"I know your works, and where you dwell, where Satan's throne is. And you hold fast to my name, and did not deny my faith even in the days in which Antipas was my faithful martyr, who was killed among you, where Satan dwells."	"I know your works, love, service, faith, and your patience; and as for your works, the last are more than the first."
Their failings	"Nevertheless I have this against you, that you have left your first love. Remember therefore from where you have fallen; repent and do the first works, or else I will come to you quickly and remove your lampstand from its place – unless you repent. But this you have, that you hate the deeds of the Nicolaitans, which I also hate."		"But I have a few things against you, because you have there those who hold the doctrine of Balaam … Thus you also have those who hold the doctrine of the Nicolaitans, which thing I hate. Repent, or else I will come to you quickly and will fight against them with the sword of my mouth."	"Nevertheless I have a few things against you, because you allow that woman Jezebel, who calls herself a prophetess, to teach and seduce my servants to commit sexual immorality and eat things sacrificed to idols … hold fast what you have till I come."
Warning	"He who has an ear, let him hear what the Spirit says to the churches."	"He who has an ear, let him hear what the Spirit says to the churches."	"He who has an ear, let him hear what the Spirit says to the churches."	"He who has an ear, let him hear what the Spirit says to the churches."
Promise	"To him who overcomes I will give to eat from the tree of life, which is in the midst of the paradise of God."	"He who overcomes shall not be hurt by the second death."	"To him who overcomes I will give some of the hidden manna to eat. And I will give him a white stone, and on the stone a new name …"	"And he who overcomes, and keeps my works until the end, to him I will give power over the nations … and I will give him the morning star."

SEVEN INTRODUCTORY LETTERS

Sardis	Philadelphia	Laodicea	Ecclesia
"These things says he who has the seven spirits of God and the seven stars:"	"These things says he who is holy, he who is true, he who has the key of David, he who opens and no one shuts, and shuts and no one opens:"	"These things says the Amen, the faithful and true witness, the beginning of the creation of God:"	Extract from opening vision
"I know your works, that you have a name that you are alive, but you are dead. Be watchful, and strengthen the things which remain, that are ready to die, for I have not found your works perfect before God. Remember therefore how you have received and heard; hold fast and repent. Therefore if you will not watch, I will come upon you as a thief, and you will not know what hour I will come upon you. You have a few names even in Sardis who have not defiled their garments; and they shall walk with me in white, for they are worthy."	"I know your works. See, I have set before you an open door, and no one can shut it; for you have a little strength, have kept my word, and have not denied my name. Indeed I will make those of the synagogue of Satan, who say they are Jews and are not, but lie – indeed I will make them come and worship before your feet, and to know that I have loved you. Because you have kept my command to persevere, I also will keep you from the hour of trial which shall come upon the whole world, to test those who dwell on the earth. Behold, I am coming quickly! Hold fast what you have, that no one may take your crown."	"I know your works, that you are neither cold nor hot. I could wish you were cold or hot. So then, because you are lukewarm, and neither cold nor hot, I will vomit you out of my mouth. Because you say, 'I am rich, have become wealthy, and have need of nothing' – and do not know that you are wretched, miserable, poor, blind, and naked – I counsel you to buy from me gold refined in the fire, that you may be rich; and white garments, that you may be clothed, that the shame of your nakedness may not be revealed; and anoint your eyes with eye salve, that you may see. As many as I love, I rebuke and chasten. Therefore be zealous and repent. Behold, I stand at the door and knock. If anyone hears my voice and opens the door, I will come in to him and dine with him, and he with me."	Jesus' assessment
			Their failings
"He who has an ear, let him hear what the Spirit says to the churches."	"He who has an ear, let him hear what the Spirit says to the churches."	"He who has an ear, let him hear what the Spirit says to the churches."	Warning
"He who overcomes shall be clothed in white garments, and I will not blot out his name from the book of life; but I will confess his name before my Father and before His angels."	"He who overcomes, I will make him a pillar in the temple of my God, and he shall go out no more. And I will write on him the name of my God and the name of the city of my God, the New Jerusalem, which comes down out of heaven from my God. And I will write on him my new name."	"To him who overcomes I will grant to sit with me on my throne, as I also overcame and sat down with my Father on His throne."	Promise

Revelation and history

The Book of Revelation is like other Bible prophecies. It speaks of events that were to occur after the message was recorded. As Revelation is the last inspired message in the Bible, there have not been any later books to show how what was prophesied in its visions actually came to pass.

Some earlier Bible prophecies are different because their fulfilment was recorded in later inspired records. Old Testament prophecies about Jesus' death and resurrection, for example, are explained in the Gospel accounts about Jesus. And there are prophecies about nations that were fulfilled within Bible times (about Babylon and Tyre, for example).

Because Revelation focuses on events that impact on Jesus' followers throughout the centuries between his first and second comings, it is history written in advance – history seen from God's perspective. Believers in each generation since the days of John have been able to see the important events of their own times portrayed in Revelation.

As we live in the days immediately before the return of Christ, we do not need to know every detail of the events that have occurred since John received the message from Jesus. But it helps to understand and appreciate the message of Revelation if we can see the links with contemporary history. Such details help:

➤ to show the accuracy of the prophecy;

➤ to encourage believers as they face difficulties that were foreseen and described in advance by Jesus.

Time periods

PROPHETICAL books often use a simple code when referring to time periods: to describe long periods of time, a day is substituted for a year. Ezekiel, for example, had to lie on his left side for 390 days and on his right side for 40 days. These symbolised the number of years when the northern and southern kingdoms of Israel and Judah would suffer attacks from the north for their iniquity (Ezekiel 4:5,6).

It is easy to understand why these two time periods were acted out symbolically by Ezekiel. It was impossible for him to lie first on one side and then on the other for over 400 *years;* he would not live that long, nor would those he was seeking to teach.

This 'day for a year' symbolism was introduced to Israel through their law (e.g., Leviticus 25:4), and by an incident when they were travelling through the wilderness. The spies who went ahead to see the fruitful land God had promised to Israel returned after 40 days and the majority only reported the difficulties that would be faced in overcoming the Canaanite inhabitants. God's response to their unfaithfulness was to condemn to death in the wilderness all the adult generation who were redeemed from Egypt:

> *"According to the number of the days in which you spied out the land, forty days, for each day you shall bear your guilt one year, namely forty years, and you shall know my rejection."*
>
> (Numbers 14:34)

When future events are described in prophecy by symbols and visions, the time periods have to be appropriate to the symbol with which they are associated, and the 'day for a year' technique is normally used.

Day for a year in Revelation

This helps us understand various passages in Revelation. In chapter 2, for example, in Jesus' letter to the believers in Smyrna, he foretold *"ten days"* of tribulation. We can now see how this indicated 10 *years*, a whole decade of persecution, which actually occurred about ten years after the message of Revelation was given, under the rule of the Roman emperor Trajan.

Twice in Revelation a much longer period of time is mentioned, 1,260 days (11:3; 12:6) – the period when two witnesses prophesy, and when the "Woman" is fed in the wilderness. As these two periods are the same length, it is probable that they occur at the same time: one thousand two hundred and sixty *years* in the history of the Christian church.

In a related passage, a time period of *"forty-two months"* is mentioned (11:2). Reckoning on the Jewish calendar, with 30 days in a month, this is equivalent to 1,260 days, and it also refers to a period of 1,260 *years*. It is related to the *"treading down of the holy city"* by Gentile nations.

Later in the same section, a different time calculation appears: *"a time and times and half a time"* (12:14). It is the period of time when the "Woman" is fed in the wilderness, previously described as 1,260 days (see verse 6). This same expression – *"a time and times and half a time"* – occurs in Daniel's prophecy (Daniel 7:25), in a passage that also deals with the conflict between the saints and the Beast. In both these passages, *"a time"* is taken to refer to a year, or 360 days. *"A time and times and half a time"* can therefore be calculated on the 'day for a year' basis as follows:

A Time (360 days)	=	360 years
Times (2 x 360 days)	=	720 years
Half a Time (180 days)	=	180 years
Total	=	1,260 years

Hour, day, month, year

In another place, a sequence of time periods occurs: an *"hour and day and month and year"* (Revelation 9:15). If the same principle of interpretation applies, this refers to 391 years:

Day	=	1 year
Month	=	30 years
Year (12 x 30)	=	360 years
Total	=	391 years

This refers to the time when the Eastern Roman Empire was attacked by powers from beyond the River Euphrates: *"Release the four angels who are bound at the great river Euphrates"* (9:14); and it ended when the city of Constantinople fell to the Turks in 1453. Exactly 391 years before this important event, in 1062, historians tell us that Mohammedan powers first started to move westwards, and crossed the River Euphrates to attack territory that was under Rome's control.

If we remember the 'day for a year' principle when we meet time periods in Revelation it will help us to understand the overall message.

Half an hour & a thousand years

But there are also other time periods in Revelation that do not seem to fit the 'day for a year' principle of interpretation:

"When he opened the seventh seal, there was silence in heaven for about half an hour." (8:1)

"The ten horns which you saw are ten kings who have received no kingdom as yet, but they receive authority for one hour as kings with the beast." (17:12)

TIME PERIODS

"And they lived and reigned with Christ for a thousand years." (20:4)

These periods are completely different from the ones marked out as *"days"*. Two are very short – *"half an hour"* and *"one hour"* – and the other is very long, *"a thousand years"*. Does the 'day for a year' principle apply here as well?

When the Bible speaks prophetically of time periods measured in years, as for example the seventy-year captivity of the nation in Babylon (Jeremiah 25:11), or the affliction of Abraham's descendants for 400 years (Genesis 15:13), they always denote *actual years*. It is thus reasonable to conclude that the thousand-year reign of Christ mentioned in Revelation 20 will last literally for 1,000 years.

Measurements of less than a year in Bible prophecies are figurative, and have to be calculated according to a formula like a 'day for a year'.

How are we to determine what is meant by there being *"silence in heaven for about half an hour"*? On the basis of a 'day for a year', it would be 15 days, and "one hour" would be 30 days. But possibly there is another technique being used here, and the 'day for a year' principle is intensified so that *"half an hour"* is actually 15 *years*, and *"one hour"* is 30 *years*.

Prophetical period	Actual time period
Years	= Actual years
Days / months	= Prophetical years, based on the principle of a 'day for a year'.
Hours	= Extending and intensifying the 'day for a year' principle.

Summary

When we encounter prophetic time periods in Revelation, three different techniques are used.

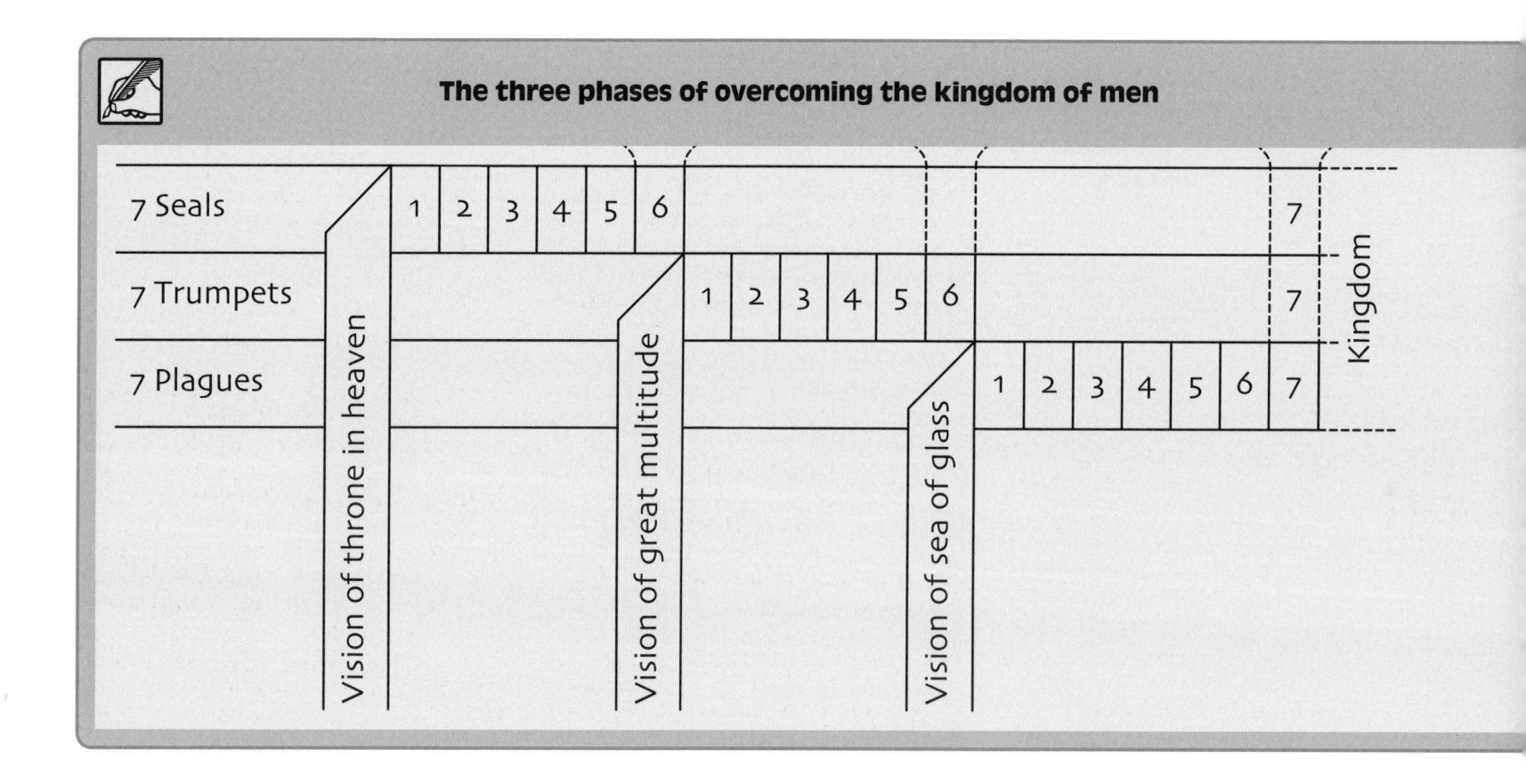

REVELATION STUDY GUIDE

The three phases of overcoming the kingdom of men

7 Seals		1	2	3	4	5	6								7	
7 Trumpets								1	2	3	4	5	6			7
7 Plagues														1	2	3	4	5	6	7

Vision of throne in heaven

Vision of great multitude

Vision of sea of glass

Kingdom

Unsealing the scroll

GREAT CHANGES IN WORLD GOVERNMENT

- **7** Seals – Judgements on pagan Rome.
- **7** Trumpets – Judgements on so-called 'Christian' Rome.
- **7** Plagues – Judgements on corrupt religion.

THE first three chapters of Revelation, as we have seen, form an introduction and overview to the whole book. Jesus' last message to his disciples shows his concern for their welfare, for he knows that because they believe in him they will be threatened by ungodly powers. The rest of the book charts the history of conflict between believers and worldly powers until Jesus returns to earth to establish God's kingdom in place of the kingdom of men.

There are three main phases in this conflict, and they are described in Revelation by three sequences of sevens, as shown in the diagram opposite: a seven-sealed scroll, seven trumpets, and seven last plagues. In common with every section of the book, each of these is introduced by a vision of the kingdom whose elements are related to the particular phase that follows the account of the vision. The seven-sealed scroll, for example, is introduced by a vision of a throne set in heaven, surrounded by living creatures and elders. The one who sits on the throne holds the seven-sealed scroll, which can be opened only by a Lamb who has been killed and made alive again.

The throne in heaven

The vision provides the key to what follows, so it must be read carefully.

John was granted the opportunity to enter "heaven" and see the *"things which must take place after this"* (Revelation 4:1; *"things which must shortly take place"*, 1:1). In the vision, these events took place "in heaven". How is this to be understood?

The prophecy of Isaiah in the Old Testament provides an answer on this occasion. It starts by addressing "the heavens" and "the earth": *"Hear, O **heavens**, and give ear, O **earth**!"* (Isaiah 1:2). Later in the chapter these terms are shown to be symbolic: *"Hear the word of the* LORD, *you **rulers** of Sodom; give ear to the law of our God, you **people** of Gomorrah"* (1:10; cp. Deuteronomy 32:1. See the chapter on signs and symbols (page 11) for details of other symbols to be found in Revelation and how to interpret them).

So, when John was shown a door open "in heaven", he was receiving information about "rulers", about government; and it was fitting that he saw a vision of God's throne, for *"the Most High rules in the kingdom of men, and gives it to whomever he chooses"* (Daniel 4:25). The vision was of the time when *"the kingdoms of this world have become the kingdoms of our Lord and of his Christ"*, for the throne was on a *"sea of glass"*. Waters in Revelation symbolise *"peoples, multitudes, nations, and tongues"* (Revelation 17:15), and they will only be still and at peace when God's glory fills the earth.

Because this is a vision of the kingdom, the throne is God's but the rulership of that age has been given to His Son. Jesus is not God, but is man *"made perfect through sufferings"* (Hebrews 2:10). This is expressed in the vision by the one on the throne looking *"like a jasper* (blue) *and a sardius* (red) *stone in appearance"* (Revelation 4:3). One of these stones represents Jesus' divine origin (blue = heaven) and the other his human descent (red = sin).

Elders and living creatures

Who then are the elders and the living creatures? Once again looking at the Old Testament can help us. Exodus 24 records the occasion when Moses was called up into Mount Sinai to receive commands from God, delivered to him by one of God's angels.

He was accompanied by Aaron, Nadab and Abihu, and 70 elders of Israel, *"and they saw the God of Israel. And there was under his feet as it were a paved work of sapphire stone, and it was like the very heavens in its clarity"* (Exodus 24:10). These men represented the nation – all of God's people who had been redeemed out of Egypt, and the angel they saw represented God in heaven.

With the elders in the vision seen by John were also four *"living creatures"*. With faces of a lion, a calf, a man and an eagle, these were like the cherubim seen by the Old Testament prophet Ezekiel (Ezekiel 1 & 10). They also had six wings and cried, *"Holy, holy, holy, Lord God Almighty"*, like the seraphim that Isaiah saw when he was granted a vision of the Lord Jesus enthroned in glory (Isaiah 6:1-8; John 12:41). Each of these Old Testament visions symbolises the relationship of true believers to the purpose of God.

So in Revelation, the elders and the living creatures represent the redeemed – not just from Israel, but from *"**every** tribe and tongue and people and nation"* (Revelation 5:9). They are clothed in white, representing righteousness (19:8), and they have golden crowns showing they have "overcome" by the blood of the Lamb.

The scroll

In the hand of the one on the throne was a scroll, *"written inside and on the back, sealed with seven seals"* (5:1). At the end of Daniel's prophecy, he was told to *"shut up the words, and seal the book until the time of the end"* (Daniel 12:4). Revelation therefore includes additional information only briefly referred to in Daniel. As Daniel received prophecies about the future destiny of God's people, the same message continues in Revelation.

We must note that the scroll was written on both sides: *"inside, and on the back"*. It therefore contained information

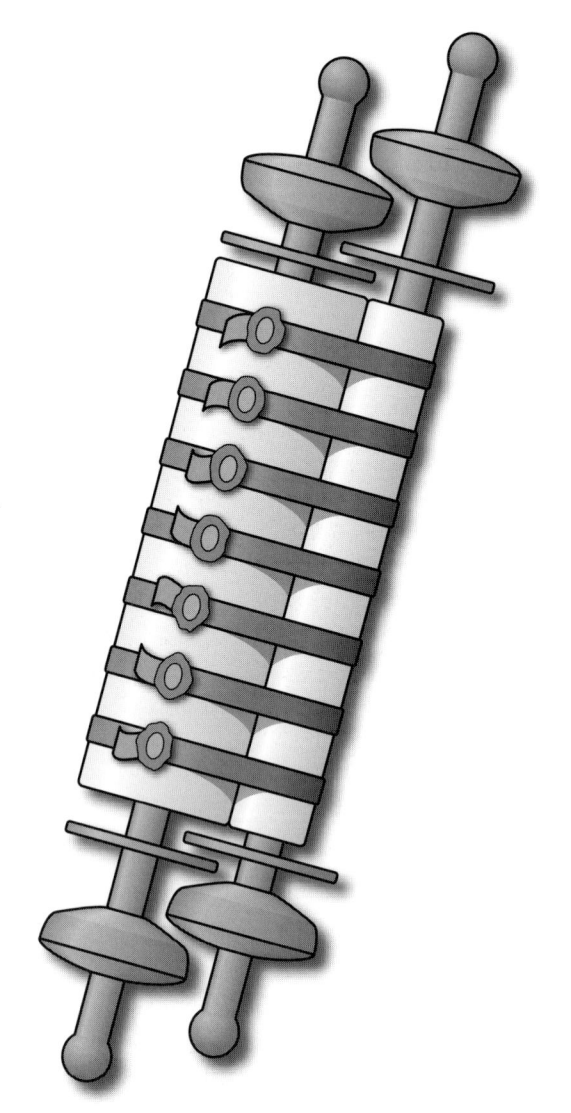

UNSEALING THE SCROLL

about events external to the believers, which would impact upon them, and upon the world in general. But it also contained information about the believers themselves: about events arising in the religious world, and which were to be important in their development.

In simple terms, these two parallel sets of unfolding events are firstly **political** – things written on the outside of the scroll; then events which are **religious** – those things written on the inside of the scroll.

As the seals are broken one by one, it is the *political events* in "heaven" that are described first.

The importance of prayer

Before considering these unfolding events, we must note how they were prompted to occur. As the Lamb takes the scroll, the elders and the living creatures fall down before him, *"each having a harp, and golden bowls full of incense, which are **the prayers of the saints**"* (Revelation 5:8).

We have seen that one of the main objectives of the book of Revelation is to *"show his* (Jesus') *servants, things which must shortly take place"* (1:1). Armed with this information, it is apparent that Jesus' disciples must pray earnestly and urgently for God's purpose to be fulfilled. The events described in Revelation 6 are the direct consequences of *"the prayers of the saints"*.

Opening the seals

In line with the features of the kingdom-vision, the events described in this section have to do with bringing the nations under God's control so that ultimately the earth will be at peace. It was necessary for the readers of Revelation to be reassured that God's power oversees all political events. History is known in advance by God, and written beforehand by His servants. Important events were gradually revealed to John as each section of the scroll was opened following the successive breaking of the seven seals.

Opening the first four seals released four horsemen into the earth. Remembering that the vision was *"in heaven"*, and that the ruling power of John's day was Roman, these events affected the people (i.e., *"the earth"*) who were living throughout the Roman Empire. Horses in scripture are usually associated with the prevailing military power (e.g., Exodus 15:1). Horses were also used by the Romans themselves to represent the power and might of Rome (see illustration alongside).

The four horses in Revelation were all different colours, and the riders carried different implements. These showed the developing character of the Roman Empire as history unfolded. The white horse and its bowman symbolised victory and peace; the red horse with a swordsman symbolised war and bloodshed; the black horse whose rider carried a pair of scales symbolised famine; and the pale horse with its deadly rider symbolised death.

The table on pages 55 and 56 contains evidence from contemporary history

Rome's military might is often depicted by horses.

indicating how accurately these symbols represented the unfolding history of Rome during the second and third centuries AD. During this period, believers in Christ had a difficult time. All around them was pagan worship, and some Caesars encouraged the persecution of any one who claimed to follow Jesus.

These successive stages of the political history of the Roman Empire were followed by a period of severe persecution for the followers of Christ – similar to the times in which John himself lived. When the fifth seal was opened, John saw *"under the altar the souls of those who had been slain for the word of God and for the testimony which they held"* (6:9, cp. 1:9 where the reason John was in exile is explained in similar terms).

Once again, the importance of prayer is emphasised. During this period of great persecution, prayers were offered to God by Jesus' faithful followers: *"**How long**, O Lord, holy and true, until you judge and avenge our blood on those who dwell on the earth?"* (6:10).

The first great earthquake

These prayers were quickly answered – but not by the return of Christ and the establishment of the kingdom, for God still had many people to call. But those cruel rulers who persecuted His people were no longer to wield power over the earth; a *"great earthquake"* would remove them, and bring different rulers into the political heavens.

This happened in the first half of the fourth century AD, when the emperor Constantine declared that Christianity would be adopted throughout the Roman Empire. The old pagan government was ended, and all future emperors claimed to be Christian.

As a result of this political "earthquake", the situation for the followers of Jesus changed radically, as it did for all who clung to the old pagan religion. The *"stars of heaven"*, or the former pagan rulers, *"fell to the earth … and the heaven* (the pagan government) *departed as a scroll when it is rolled up"* (6:13,14).

One of the effects of this "great earthquake" was a shift in the empire's centre. When Constantine became sole ruler, he moved his headquarters to the ancient city of Byzantium, situated at the junction of Europe and Asia, and renamed it Constantinople. There was no doubting his intentions: to unite East and West under one supreme ruler.

While all these events were occurring in the political "heavens", we must not forget that the scroll that foretold them also had information written on the inside. This means that there is further information in Revelation about these events, but it is shown from a religious and not a political viewpoint (see later chapter 16 – page 63).

But before we leave the seven-sealed scroll we must note the remarkable accuracy of this section of the prophecy. The information was revealed to John before the end of the first century AD, and it concerned events that would unfold during the following 250 years. Secular historians have confirmed that the various stages of the Roman Empire during that period are faithfully recorded by the symbols used in the seven seals' prophecy. The reader thus has great confidence to move on to later chapters, where the events described were even farther removed from John's day.

Mosaic depicting Constantine choosing Byzantium as his new capital city.

First seal

"And I looked, and behold, a white horse. He who sat on it had a bow; and a crown was given to him, and he went out conquering and to conquer." (Revelation 6:2)

- White indicates a time of relative peace. Note that in the next seal period, peace is taken away (verse 4).
- The rider was given a crown (Greek, *stephanos*, the wreath or garland given as a prize to victors in public games).
- This period of comparative peace allowed Christianity to spread widely throughout the Empire.

Second seal

"Another horse, fiery red, went out. And it was granted to the one who sat on it to take peace from the earth, and that people should kill one another; and there was given to him a great sword." (verse 4)

- Red indicates bloodshed. Note that peace was taken away, and people killed each other.
- The *"great sword"* (Greek, *machaira*) was literally a short sword or dagger – an assassin's, not a soldier's weapon.

A period of civil war beset the Empire at the end of the 2nd century AD. Emperors were assassinated and national resources were squandered.

Third seal

"Behold, a black horse, and he who sat on it had a pair of scales in his hand. And I heard a voice in the midst of the four living creatures saying, 'A quart of wheat for a denarius, and three quarts of barley for a denarius; and do not harm the oil and the wine.'" (verses 5,6)

- Black indicates famine and distress, hence the reference to wheat, oil and wine, and to the balances.

The Emperor Caracalla (AD212-217) continued to squander the Empire's resources of food, and imposed such high taxes that farming became unprofitable.

Fourth seal

"Behold, a pale horse. And the name of him who sat on it was Death, and Hades followed with him. And power was given to them over a fourth of the earth, to kill with sword, with hunger, with death, and by the beasts of the earth." (verse 8)

- The horse was *"pale"* (Greek, *chloros*, sickly or green), indicating mortal sickness. *"Hades"* is the grave.
- *"A fourth of the earth"*, i.e., of the Empire.
- *"Beasts of the earth"*: wild animals often symbolise barbaric peoples, and during this period the Germans, Samartians, Allemani and Goths invaded the Empire.
- The Empire was decimated: half the population died – through wars, the tyranny of various emperors, pestilence and famine. A plague (AD250-265) raged through the

Empire. At its height it killed 5,000 people a day in Rome.

Fifth seal

"When he opened the fifth seal, I saw under the altar the souls of those who had been slain for the word of God and for the testimony which they held. And they cried with a loud voice, saying, 'How long, O Lord, holy and true, until you judge and avenge our blood on those who dwell on the earth?' Then a white robe was given to each of them; and it was said to them that they should rest a little while longer, until both the number of their fellow servants and their brethren, who would be killed as they were, was completed."

(Revelation 6:9-11)

- A period of severe persecution for Christians. The symbol of an altar is used in Hebrews 13:10 of Jesus Christ, so "the souls under the altar" are people who belong to, or are under, the protection of Jesus.

Sixth seal

"Behold, there was a great earthquake; and the sun became black as sackcloth of hair, and the moon became like blood. And the stars of heaven fell to the earth, as a fig tree drops its late figs when it is shaken by a mighty wind. Then the sky receded as a scroll when it is rolled up, and every mountain and island was moved out of its place. And the kings of the earth, the great men, the rich men, the commanders, the mighty men, every slave and every free man, hid themselves in the caves and in the rocks of the mountains, and said to the mountains and rocks, 'Fall on us and hide us from the face of him who sits on the throne and from the wrath of the Lamb!'"

(Revelation 6:12-16)

- The "Great Earthquake" affected the ruling powers who were frightened by the *"wrath of the Lamb"* when existing political and religious systems were overthrown. The Emperor Constantine made a debased form of Christianity the state religion by the Edict of Mediolanum (Milan) in AD313.

On the death of Diocletian there were four ruling generals: two in the west and two in the east. On defeating Maxentius at the Milvian Bridge, the new emperor in the West was Constantine I, The Great (AD312-327); Licinius was emperor in the East until his death (in AD324), leaving Constantine as sole ruler over the entire Empire.

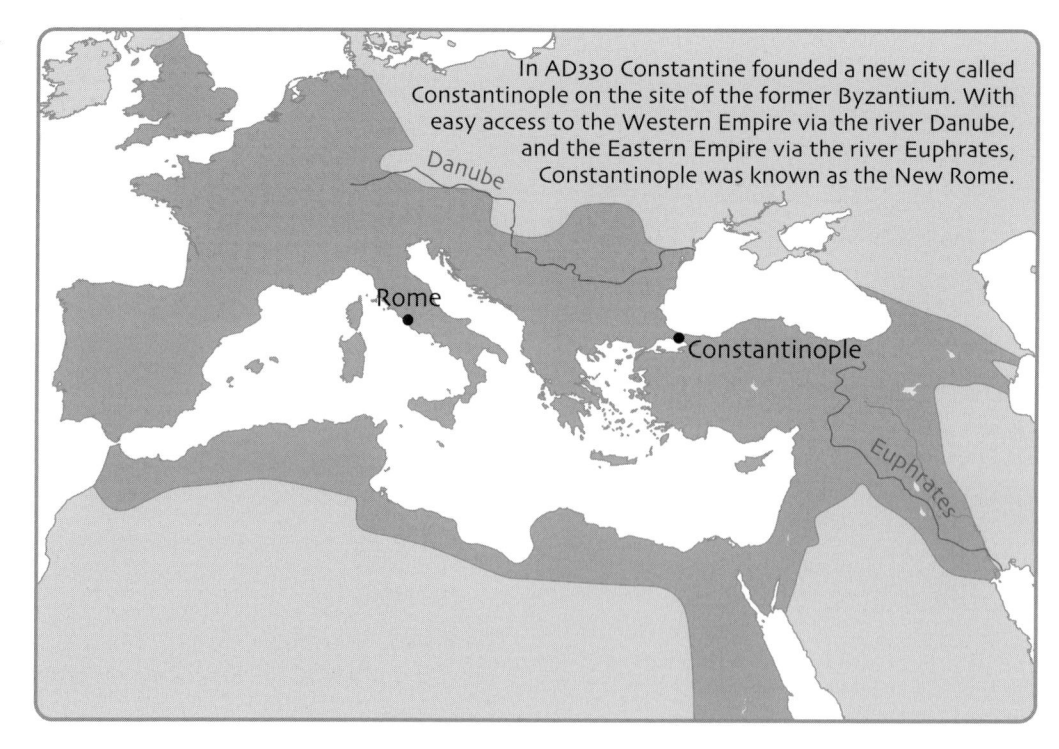

In AD330 Constantine founded a new city called Constantinople on the site of the former Byzantium. With easy access to the Western Empire via the river Danube, and the Eastern Empire via the river Euphrates, Constantinople was known as the New Rome.

Seven trumpets

CALLING NATIONS TO BATTLE

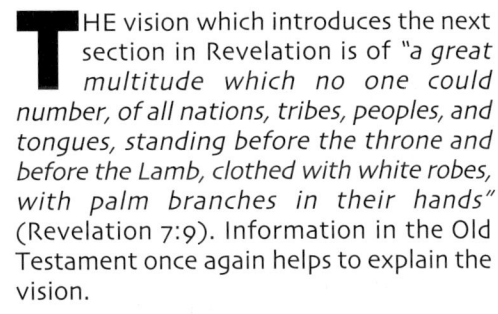

THE vision which introduces the next section in Revelation is of *"a great multitude which no one could number, of all nations, tribes, peoples, and tongues, standing before the throne and before the Lamb, clothed with white robes, with palm branches in their hands"* (Revelation 7:9). Information in the Old Testament once again helps to explain the vision.

The Feast of Tabernacles

The nation of Israel carried branches from palm trees once every year when they celebrated the Feast of Tabernacles in the seventh month. During this feast they remembered the deliverance of their ancestors from Egypt and their wandering through the wilderness on the way to the promised land.

The palm branches were used to build 'booths' or tabernacles, in which they camped during the seven days of the feast. We should note how the feast was in the **seventh** month, and lasted for **seven** days, looking forward to the great Seventh Day when the kingdom will be the Lord's. The three great characteristics of the Feast of Tabernacles make it apparent that it taught the nation of Israel about the coming kingdom: there was "great rejoicing", there was "great abundance", and they relied wholly on God for their protection.

God looked after His people in the wilderness, and the same will be true of the kingdom age, but to an even greater extent. Notice how the language of Revelation 7 builds on the nation's wilderness experiences:

"These are the ones who come out of the great tribulation, and washed their robes and made them white in the blood of the Lamb ... They shall neither hunger any more nor thirst any more; the sun shall not strike them, nor any heat; for the Lamb who is in the midst of the throne will shepherd them and lead them to living fountains of waters. And God will wipe away every tear from their eyes." (verses 14-17)

The seventh month

This Old Testament background is further emphasised by the details of the Jewish calendar. The Feast of Tabernacles (starting on the 15th day of the seventh month) was preceded by the Day of Atonement (10th day), when the nation remembered God's mercy in forgiving their sins and, right at the start of the seventh month, by the Feast of Trumpets.

In just the same way, in Revelation the kingdom vision based on the Feast of Tabernacles describes events that are preceded by a sequence of seven trumpets, and then by the return of Christ when those who have been redeemed are finally restored to God "for his sake".

In the vision this work starts with the nation of Israel. The twelve tribes of Jacob who hold "the hope of Israel", have God's seal in their foreheads or their minds. For, *"faith comes by hearing, and hearing by the word of God"* (Romans 10:17). The sealing of believers in their minds is in great contrast to the work of the Beast, whose mark sealed the foreheads of all who were deceived by his teachings (see Revelation 13:16).

In the previous vision (in chapters 4 & 5), we were introduced to believers *"out of every tribe and tongue and people and nation"* (5:9). Now we are told that this great company includes many that come *"out of great tribulation"*, and the trumpets section explains how this tribulation occurred.

Once more, we note that the events represented by the seven trumpets were God's response to the prayers of the saints:

> "the smoke of the incense, with the prayers of the saints, ascended before God from the angel's hand … So the seven angels who had the seven trumpets prepared themselves to sound." (8:4-6)

The seven trumpets are in two distinct phases. Firstly, four trumpets bring distress successively on earth and heavens – i.e., peoples and rulers (see pages 12 and 51). In each case, a third was destroyed, indicating the effect of military attacks on the Roman Empire, which at this stage in its development was divided roughly into three parts (see map on page 60). It was usual for armies to be called to battle by trumpeters, so the symbol is very apt, as well as reminding us of the destruction of Jericho by Israel as they entered the promised land.

We are able to see clearly in these events the barbarian attacks on Rome – mainly on the Western Empire. Over a period of time, the Roman Empire had become corrupt and degraded. The army was no longer invincible, and its cities and organisation were attractive to the people and tribes living in the surrounding territories.

The "woe" trumpets

The second phase (trumpets 5-7) was different. An angel was seen by John *"flying through the midst of heaven, saying with a loud voice, Woe, woe, woe to the inhabitants of the earth, because of the remaining blasts of the trumpet of the three angels who are about to sound!"* (8:13).

The first four trumpets represented events in the West; the next trumpets concern the Eastern Empire. Attacks on this part came from a completely different and unexpected source: from *"the bottomless pit, and smoke arose out of the*

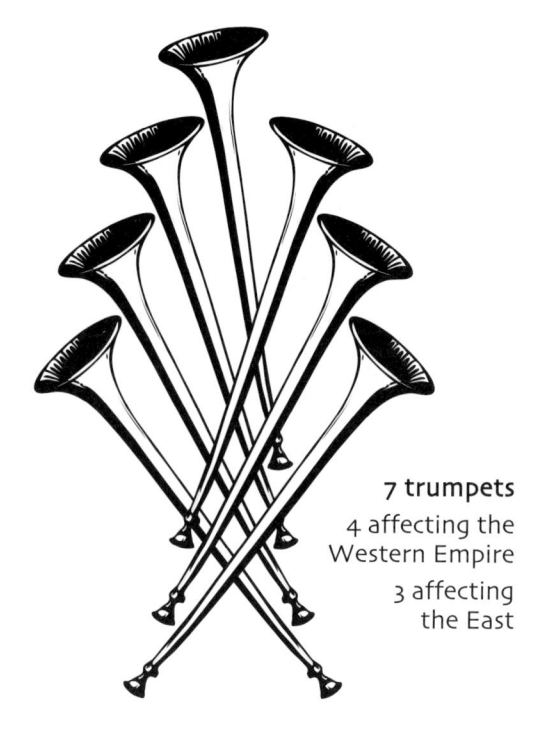

The seventh month in Israel's calendar

Day	Event
1	Feast of Trumpets
10	Day of Atonement
15 – 22	Feast of Tabernacles

7 trumpets
4 affecting the Western Empire
3 affecting the East

pit like the smoke of a great furnace. So the sun and the air were darkened because of the smoke of the pit" (9:2).

The bottomless pit is somewhere 'without bounds that cannot be fathomed' (see panel on page 62), and in Revelation refers to areas outside the boundaries of the kingdom – either the kingdom of men, as in this section, or the kingdom of God, as it occurs in a later passage in the book (20:3).

The three trumpets that sounded *"Woe, woe, woe to the inhabitants of the earth"* (8:13), called forth armies that attacked mainly the Eastern section of the Roman Empire centred on Constantinople. Saracens, Mongols, Ottomans and Turks all tried to establish their power in the area where Rome's rule held sway.

What was the effect of all these attacks on the different parts of the Roman Empire? *"The rest of mankind, who were not killed by these plagues, did not repent of the works of their hands, that they should not worship demons, and idols of gold, silver, brass, stone, and wood, which can neither see nor hear nor walk"* (9:20).

This explains that the waves of attacks on the Empire had an underlying purpose – to warn the inhabitants to turn from idolatry and worship God. But the warnings were not heeded. Idolatry was still rampant; the commands of God were ignored, and His people were persecuted. Before the seventh angel could sound his trumpet (11:15), another great earthquake occurred when the "names" or titles of men were abolished (verse 13, KJV margin).

Another prophecy of God was being fulfilled by these invasions from the East. God's land, promised to Abraham and his faithful descendants *"for ever"* was once again overrun. The Jews were first scattered after the days of Jesus by the Romans, who destroyed Jerusalem and drove its inhabitants into foreign lands. Palestine soon fell under the control of Eastern powers, and they used its territory when they invaded the Roman Empire, constantly passing over it and treading it down.

The second great earthquake

Though ostensibly 'Christian' during the trumpet period, the Roman Empire failed to uphold God's laws. Its leaders were particularly to blame, having elevated themselves above the people for purposes of power and greed. The second "great earthquake" brought to an end all these abuses when the people removed the aristocrats, princes, kings, nobles and priests (i.e., the names and titles of men) who had oppressed them.

In the *"great earthquake, a tenth of the city fell"* (Revelation 11:13). The *"great city"* of the kingdom of men had ten parts, just as the Beast had ten horns or kingdoms (17:12), and Nebuchadnezzar's image had toes that represented the mixed powers of the degraded Roman empire. The downfall of the 'Christianised' empire started in one of these ten parts. The French Revolution in 1789 was the most momentous incident in a movement that completely changed the face of the political world. The change was as drastic as when Rome formally adopted Christianity. The earthquake decisively ended the old era, and ushered in a new one.

In considering these events, we must not forget the vision that introduced them. God's faithful followers retained their faith by setting their minds on His word of truth. During "great tribulation", they *"washed their robes and made them white in the blood of the Lamb"* (7:14).

The second great earthquake

"There is a universal quality about the French Revolution which does not pertain to any of Europe's many other convulsions. Indeed, this was the event which gave the word 'Revolution' its full, modern meaning: that is, no mere political upheaval, but the complete overthrow of a system of government together with its social, economic and cultural foundations."

Norman Davies, *Europe: a History*, Oxford, 1996

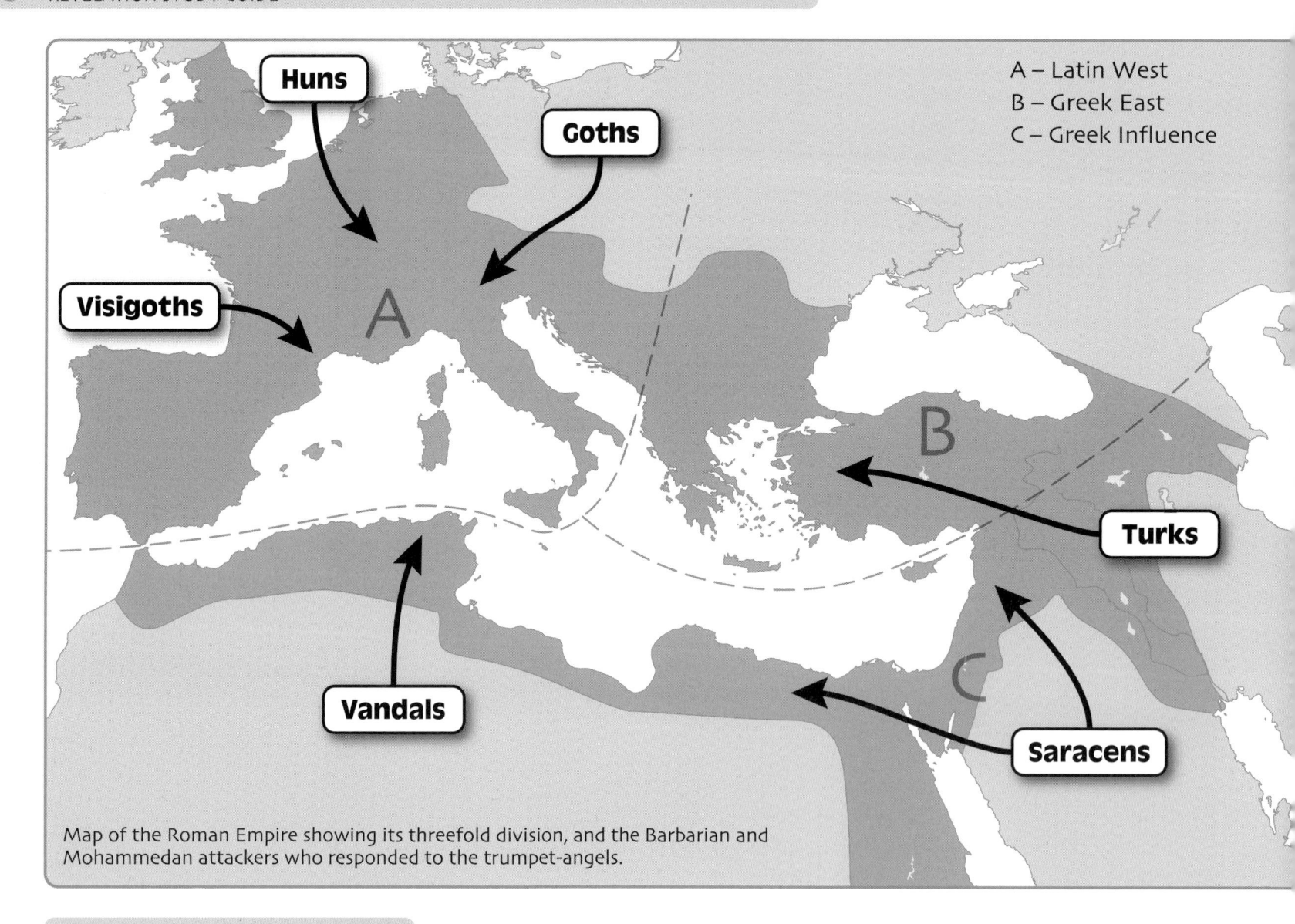

REVELATION STUDY GUIDE

A – Latin West
B – Greek East
C – Greek Influence

Huns
Goths
Visigoths
Vandals
Turks
Saracens

Map of the Roman Empire showing its threefold division, and the Barbarian and Mohammedan attackers who responded to the trumpet-angels.

Seven trumpets – invasions from beyond Rome's borders

Barbarian attacks on the Western Empire (Trumpets 1-4)

1. Alaric & the Visigoths attack Western third of the empire (AD395):

> "The first angel sounded: and hail and fire followed, mingled with blood, and they were thrown to the earth. And a third of the trees were burned up, and all green grass was burned up." (Revelation 8:7)

2. Genseric & the Vandals use naval warfare (AD429):

> "The second angel sounded: and something like a great mountain burning with fire was thrown into the sea, and a third of the sea became blood. And a third of the living creatures in the sea died, and a third of the ships were destroyed." (Revelation 8:8,9)

3. Attila & the Huns destroy leading cities (AD451):

> "The third angel sounded: and a great star fell from heaven, burning like a torch, and it fell on a third of the rivers and on the springs of water. The name of the star is Wormwood. A third of the waters became wormwood, and many men died from the water, because it was made bitter." (Revelation 8:10,11)

4. Goths invade and put their king, Theodoric, on the throne (AD493):

> "The fourth angel sounded: and a third of the sun was struck, a third of the moon, and a third of the stars, so that a third of them were darkened. A third of the day did not shine, and likewise the night." (Revelation 8:12)

Mohammedan attacks on the Eastern Empire (Trumpets 5 & 6)

5. Mahomet and the Saracens (AD622-932).

Mahomet fled from Mecca to Medina in AD622. Within 100 years Palestine, Syria, Egypt, North Africa and Spain were Moslem countries:

> "The fifth angel sounded: and I saw a star fallen from heaven to the earth. To him was given the key to the bottomless pit. And he opened the bottomless pit, and smoke arose out of the pit like the smoke of a great furnace ... out of the smoke locusts came upon the earth ... On their heads were crowns of something like gold, and their faces were like the faces of men. They had hair like women's hair, and their teeth were like lions' teeth ... They had tails like scorpions, and there were stings in their tails. Their power was to hurt men five months. And they had as king over them the angel of the bottomless pit, whose name in Hebrew is Abaddon, but in Greek he has the name Apollyon." (Revelation 9:1-11)

6. The Turks (AD1062-1453)

Constantinople, capital of the Eastern Roman Empire, was captured by Mohammed II in AD1453:

> "The sixth angel sounded ... 'Release the four angels who are bound at the great river Euphrates.' So the four angels, who had been prepared for the hour and day and month and year, were released to kill a third of mankind ... out of their mouths came fire, smoke, and brimstone. By these three plagues a third of mankind was killed ... But the rest of mankind, who were not killed by these plagues, did not repent of the works of their hands, that they should not worship demons, and idols of gold, silver, brass, stone, and wood, which can neither see nor hear nor walk. And they did not repent of their murders or their sorceries or their sexual immorality or their thefts." (Revelation 9:13-21)

The bottomless pit

ONE of the recurring symbols in Revelation is "the bottomless pit", and it will help us understand the book's message if we can find out more about what this symbol represents.

"The bottomless pit" (Greek, *abussos*) gives us our word 'abyss'. Literally, it means 'unbounded', and is used in Revelation to refer to anything that cannot be fathomed; hence "the bottomless pit".

So dominant was the power and rule of Rome that all peoples who did not live within the borders of the Empire were considered to be barbarians. The areas where these different people lived had not been conquered by Rome, nor by many of the preceding world powers. It was very reasonable therefore to describe where they lived as the "bottomless pit": a boundless area, beyond the borders of the Empire.

The term is first used in Revelation 9 during the period of the fifth trumpet. When it sounded, a "star" who had been given its key opened the bottomless pit. As "the heavens" symbolise rulership, and the sun, moon and stars the individual rulers, this "star" indicates a ruler through whose work the inhabitants of "the bottomless pit" entered the area ruled over by the Beast.

This leader (called "Abaddon" in Hebrew and "Appolyon" in Greek), was "The Destroyer" who led his forces against the powers of the Beast. These forces were the Saracens whose vast empire bordered Rome's to the east and south-east.

The Beast from the bottomless pit

Later references to "the bottomless pit" relate it to the Beast itself, and not to those who invaded the Beast's territory. The first time the Beast is mentioned in Revelation, it is described as *"the beast that ascends out of the bottomless pit"*, who makes war against God's witnesses (11:7).

In one phase of its development therefore, the Beast's power originated from the barbarian areas, and not from within the boundaries of the Roman Empire. This actually happened as Rome began to decline. The decline and fall of the Roman Empire (the title of a well-known account of the downfall of Rome by the 18th century historian Edward Gibbon) occurred from two sources: internal corruption and immorality, and external attacks by barbarian tribes. Gradually, Rome's power fell to the barbarians, so it was true to say that the Beast ascended (i.e., came to political power) from "the bottomless pit" – the territory outside the Roman Empire.

This situation was repeated later in the history of the Beast, so that it is described in chapter 17 as: *"The beast that was, and is not, and will ascend out of the bottomless pit and go to perdition"* (17:8). The beast's power will not always arise from within the borders of the Empire; sometimes it will come from "the bottomless pit" of barbarian countries.

What this verse in Revelation 17 also tells us is that "the bottomless pit" does not describe the grave or death. For the Beast has to come out of the bottomless pit in order to go to perdition, or final extinction.

At the end of Revelation, an angel has the key of the bottomless pit where he imprisons the Dragon (20:1-3). This is a complete reversal of what happened before. The Dragon is the original Beast from which all the others developed: they always had the Dragon's power or authority; they spoke "as a dragon". These verses tell us that when Jesus returns, the Dragon will be banished from God's kingdom. It will be placed in "the bottomless pit", from where it will be impossible to continue deceiving the nations of the earth. Because the Dragon here refers to the antagonistic attitude towards God that characterised many human governments, it is that attitude which will be banished from God's kingdom. So here, the "bottomless pit" is not a geographical reference.

16

The witnesses

LIVING THROUGH THE SECOND GREAT EARTHQUAKE

EARTHQUAKES are dangerous times for those who live through them. The next section of Revelation starts by considering the impact on believers of the events symbolised by the trumpets, and by the second "great earthquake".

John is then also shown the effects of the other two great earthquakes. The impact of the second great earthquake is shown in chapter 11; the events surrounding the first great earthquake are revealed in Revelation 12; and those surrounding the third great earthquake appear in chapters 17 & 18.

At the end of the trumpets

By the time we reach Revelation 10, two of the three great judgement sequences in Revelation have been described: the seals and the trumpets. These reveal events that mainly involve the political "heavens", though people living on the earth were obviously affected by them. In the section starting in chapter 10, the focus changes: *"I saw still another mighty angel* **coming down from heaven***, clothed with a cloud. And a rainbow was on his head, his face was like the sun, and his feet like pillars of fire. He had a little book open in his hand. And he set his right foot on the sea and his left foot on the land"* (Revelation 10:1,2).

There can be little doubt that this vision is closely related to the opening vision in Revelation of *"one like the Son of Man"* whose *"eyes were like a flame of fire; his feet were like fine brass, as if refined in a furnace"* (1:14,15). But now the interest is directed towards the earth: the "sea" and the "land", i.e., the people who are being ruled by human princes, kings and governors.

Religious events

We were prepared for this change when we noted that the seven-sealed scroll, seen when *"a door was opened in heaven"*, was *"written inside* **and on the back**" (5:1, see page 36). It is now time for the scroll to be turned over to reveal what life is like in the kingdom of men for believers in Jesus – i.e., *"on earth"*.

The message is encouraging, for the angel explains that the sounding of the seventh trumpet will herald the end of *"the mystery of God ... as he declared to his servants the prophets"* (10:7). This confirms that the seven last plagues, which are all contained in the seventh trumpet period, form **the final judgements** on the kingdom of men before God intervenes by sending the Lord Jesus Christ back to the earth.

Much was achieved as *"the mystery of God"* unfolded. Pagan Rome, responsible for crucifying the Lord Jesus Christ and persecuting his followers, was subjected to various judgements that led to the first *"great earthquake"*. The character of the empire changed overnight; it was 'Christianised', and an attempt was made to unite it under a single emperor ruling from Constantinople, the meeting point of Asia and Europe. But this phase of the fourth beast's dominion was also subject to judgement: the barbarians attacked in the West, placing their king on the throne in Rome; and the Saracens and Turks attacked from the East, eventually capturing Constantinople.

Unbroken line of testimony

During these two great epochs (seals and trumpets), there was a consistent witness to the truth about Jesus. John himself *"bore witness to the word of God, and to the testimony of Jesus Christ"* (1:2). And after his death, there were others who continued his testimony, forming an unbroken chain (see 6:9; 12:17; 14:12 & 19:9,10). Through their work, the number of saints increased. But the task was not always pleasant, as John himself learned: *"I took the little book out of the angel's hand and ate it, and it was as sweet as honey in my mouth. But when I had eaten it, my stomach became bitter. And he said to me, 'You must prophesy again about many peoples, nations, tongues, and kings'"* (10:10,11).

What would be the result of all this witnessing? John was told to *"Rise and measure the temple of God, the altar, and those who worship there"* (11:1). The temple is where the redeemed saints are found (see 7:14,15). They form *"the holy city"* (cp. 21:2), which is being developed out of *"strangers and sojourners"* living in *"the great city"* of mankind (see Hebrews 11:9,10). John was being told that believers would continue to be *"added unto the Lord"* (Acts 5:14).

But this was not going to happen painlessly: *"the holy city"* of believers was to be *"given to the Gentiles. And they will tread it underfoot for forty-two months"* (Revelation 11:2). This is equivalent to 1,260 years (42 months of 30 days each; see chapter on "Time periods", page 47). This is why in a previous vision there were *"under the altar the souls of those who had been slain for the word of God and for the testimony which they held"* (6:9). Life was not easy for Jesus' followers, either in pagan Rome or in 'Christianised' Rome.

The 1,260 years when the believers were trodden underfoot relates most appropriately to the period beginning with the formation of the so-called "universal church", which claimed prominence over all other Christian churches. This period of time is roughly equivalent to the period covered by the first six trumpet judgements. True believers were subject to persecution

THE WITNESSES

and ridicule, and only a few brave witnesses stood up against the mighty power of Rome.

During the sixth trumpet

A significant development in this chain of faithful witnesses is described in Revelation 11, which occurs during the period when the sixth trumpet sounds (see 11:14). The message focuses on this particular age, as it is an important example of how "religion" and "politics" interact.

Two specific groups of witnesses are identified. We are also given the following information about them:

- They are described as olive trees (oil represents a motivating philosophy, like God's word);
- and as lampstands (lit by that philosophy);
- fire goes out of their mouth to devour their enemies (when they speak about God's coming judgements);
- they have power to bring drought, to turn rivers into blood, and to plague the earth (God's judgements upon those who do not bow to His will).

To anyone familiar with the Old Testament scriptures, this vision is very similar to one in Zechariah's prophecy, when he saw a lampstand and two olive trees. Zechariah prophesied at a time when God's people needed encouragement if they were to remain true to God's word. The vision showed that their two leaders (Zerubbabel a prince, and Joshua a priest) were *"anointed to serve the LORD of all the earth"* (Zechariah 4:14, NIV). Both these leaders were motivated by the same principles, and worked towards the same end – shown by the oil feeding a single lampstand.

Similar symbols are used in Revelation 11, but with some significant differences. There are two witnesses in Revelation (one political, one religious), but their motivation is different despite the apparent similarity of their aims (this is indicated by the presence of **two** lampstands in Revelation, as well as two olive trees). Both witnesses oppose the Beast: one from political motives, and the other because of religious persecution.

Not completely destroyed

John was shown that the Beast will destroy both these witnesses. The same pattern is followed here as when Jesus was crucified. Rome and the Jewish leaders thought they had killed Jesus, but three days later he rose again. When the witnesses are killed, the Beast again thinks he is victorious, and so do many of the people on earth who were unhappy with the witnesses' message.

But, just as Jesus rose from death, so the witnesses were not silenced: *"After three-and-a-half days the breath of life from God entered them, and they stood on their feet, and great fear fell on those who saw them … And* **they ascended to heaven** *in a cloud, and their enemies saw them"* (Revelation 11:11,12).

As we have seen, this event occurred at the end of the sixth trumpet period, and led directly to the second *"great earthquake"*. Some of those who opposed the corruption of Christianised Rome ascended into the political heavens: *"In the same hour there was a great earthquake, and a tenth of the city fell. In the earthquake seven thousand people were killed, and the rest were afraid and gave glory to the God of heaven"* (verse 13).

Overcoming tyranny

We considered in the previous chapter how, in the 18th century, great revolutionary movements swept across the civilised world, deposing priests, princes, kings and governors. There were basically two forms of opposition to the long tyranny of the Middle Ages: political and religious. There was a genuine uprising of the common people who had been oppressed for centuries; they were led by reformers, some of whom sought political power themselves, and who were prepared to use force to achieve their ends. Their philosophy was politically motivated, and all-pervading.

But there were also others whose consciences were deeply troubled by the religion of fear and corruption falsely represented as the gospel of Christ. The aims of these two groups briefly coincided, and opportunity arose to witness against the excesses of the Beast.

Some of those who saw through the false claims of the deposed kings, princes and priests, came to power after their removal: *"they ascended to heaven"* – i.e., to a position of political power. It seemed at the time as if this could be the impetus for Christ's return. But another sequence of judgements, symbolised by seven bowls containing *"the seven **last** plagues"* (15:1), was still to come.

But before Revelation describes the pouring out of these judgements, more information is revealed about the Beast and believers in Christ to prepare us for the nature of the kingdom of men upon which the seven last plagues must fall.

More about the Beast

THE RELIGIOUS DIMENSION

THE development of the Beast has already been considered briefly, but we now need to look more carefully at the later stages. This was what Daniel was so keen to understand. He wanted *"to know the truth about the fourth beast ... and the ten horns that were on its head, and the other horn which came up, before which three fell, namely, that horn which had eyes and a mouth which spoke pompous words, whose appearance was greater than his fellows"* (Daniel 7:19,20).

Some of this development was revealed to Daniel in successive visions recorded in his prophecy (see page 21), helping to prepare us for the continuing saga of the Beast as it passes through different phases in Revelation. Daniel's visions are therefore expanded in Revelation, as shown in diagrammatic form overleaf.

Daniel saw the fourth great power (Rome) divided into two – an Eastern and Western 'leg' on Nebuchadnezzar's image. He saw it incorporate the territories of ten former nations in the ten-horned Beast revealed to him in a dream. He saw three of these horns destroyed by one that grew to have eyes and a mouth like a man.

In just the same way, John saw the Beast develop and change to suit the circumstances.

If we are also to understand these later developments, it is necessary first of all to learn more about the character of the Beast. The subject is introduced in chapter 12. This passage creates a problem in the minds of many readers. If it is read out of context, it seems to be describing the birth of Jesus to the Israelite maid, Mary. But Revelation, as we have already noted, only deals with events from the time when John first received the message from Jesus through to the establishment of the kingdom of God. It does not describe past events. Revelation 12 describes the Beast and how it responded to followers of the Lord Jesus Christ, who are depicted as a "Woman".

A Woman clothed with the sun

In the Bible, women are used to represent both faithful and unfaithful religious groups. The Apostle Paul speaks of the Church as the wife of the Lord Jesus Christ (Ephesians 5:32), and of presenting faithful believers *"as a chaste virgin to Christ"* (2 Corinthians 11:2).

But believers do not always remain faithful, and the history of the Christian

17 REVELATION STUDY GUIDE

Daniel's Fourth Beast as it appears first in Revelation is a "great red Dragon", which directly opposes the "Woman" – religious ideas allied to political aspirations

| Daniel 2 | Daniel 7 | Daniel 8 | Revelation 12 |

68

17 MORE ABOUT THE BEAST

In Revelation 13 the Beast reveals its connections with the beasts that Daniel saw. It combines features from Babylon, Persia, Greece and Rome.

Later still it pretends to be lamb-like and seeks to perpetuate that image.

Revelation 13

But the religious aspect is deceitful. The Beast is blasphemous; it is a False Prophet.

Revelation 16

All deceit is stripped away when the Beast is revealed being ridden by the fallen and degraded Woman. An apostate religious system now controls the kingdom of men.

Revelation 17

69

church throughout the centuries since John received the Revelation is largely a story of failure. The word of God was soon replaced by the opinions of men. Instead of being motivated by love, men became power-hungry. They were prepared to use religion as a cloak for ungodliness. As time passed, the *"chaste virgin"* grew coarse and lewd, and became the blasphemous prostitute pictured in the vision in Revelation 17 – just as Israel did in Old Testament times (see Ezekiel 16).

Woman "with child"

The Woman in Revelation 12 is at a much earlier stage in her development. She will never be a completely *"chaste virgin"* until Jesus separates the unfaithful from the faithful disciples. Even the first century ecclesias had their Jezebels, as we learn from the letters to the seven ecclesias in Asia in chapters 2 & 3. The Woman in this vision is an aggregate picture of all Jesus' followers – the 'Church' of those days – and she had been unfaithful to her Lord, for she was *"with child"*.

She was seen *"in heaven"*; she was *"clothed with the sun, with the moon under her feet"*, and she was crowned with *"twelve stars"*. These symbols all represent rulership; the heavens are the government, the sun is the principal ruler, the moon the religious authority and the stars are princes (see chapter on "Signs and symbols", page 11).

We need therefore to ask when 'the Church' could be seen in the political "heavens". This did not happen until Christianity became the state religion of the Roman Empire. The vision therefore gives further details about the first *"great earthquake"* in the time of the emperor Constantine, when he introduced Christianity as the imperial religion.

The man of sin

The Beast started its career in Revelation as a purely political power persecuting the followers of Jesus. But as time passed, a strange change occurred: it pretended to worship Jesus itself and claimed to be his representative on earth – it was *"like a lamb"*, but it still *"spoke like a dragon"*.

This was foreseen right at the beginning, when the Dragon waited to devour the child which was to be born to the Woman. It was not allowed to destroy the child, who became the ruler of the kingdom of men: he was *"caught up to God and his throne"* (Revelation 12:5) – in this case, the throne from which God rules in the kingdom of men (Daniel 4:17).

This symbolic language describes how the Empire adopted Christianity, but its policies were still those of the Dragon. Christianity was merely a cloak. Nothing had really changed. The Beast so completely pretended to be Christian, that everything to do with it masqueraded as if it was Godly. Revelation therefore sounds a warning to the true followers of Jesus, lest they be deceived: *"Here is wisdom. Let him who has understanding calculate the number of the beast, for it is the number of **a man**:*

"Now a great sign appeared in heaven: a woman clothed with the sun, with the moon under her feet, and on her head a garland of twelve stars ... bore a male Child who was to rule all nations with a rod of iron ..."
(Revelation 12:1,5).

MORE ABOUT THE BEAST

> ### Number 666 in the Bible
>
> Revelation, as we have seen is all built round the number seven, which stands for completeness, and looks forward to the great Day of God's Rest.
>
> By contrast, the number six is always associated with man. Adam was created in the 6th day and Goliath – the original "man of sin" was over 6 cubits tall, and had a spear whose head weighed six hundred shekels of iron (1 Samuel 17:4-7).
>
> The golden image made by Nebuchadnezzar, after he saw a dream of the kingdom of men represented as a great metallic figure, was 60 cubits high and 6 cubits broad (Daniel 3:1).
>
> The Beast having the number 666 therefore represents the kingdom of men.
>
> The Romans did not use the Arabic numbers we use (1, 2, 3, 4, etc.), but a system they developed themselves: I=1, V=5, X=10, L=50, C=100, D=500 & M=1,000. Romans would write the number 666 by using just one of the first six of these symbols: DCLXVI.
>
> The last Roman 'number' M, the seventh, is equivalent to 1,000. Does this relate to God's seventh day when His earth will be at rest?

His number is six hundred and sixty-six" (Revelation 13:18). For the meaning of this number, see the panel alongside.

The *"man child"* was the product of Christianity and elevated to rulership of the kingdom of men – rulers claiming to operate on the basis of Christian ethics. Yet the individual rulers were still Roman emperors. The Man Child escaped persecution by the Dragon of all who claimed to follow the Lord Jesus Christ, but he quickly assumed the character of the Beast, for he began to *"rule all nations with a rod of iron"* (Revelation 12:5).

This tells us two things about the Man Child:

- he pretended to be like Christ, whom the Psalmist says will *"break (the nations) with a rod of iron; you shall dash them to pieces like a potter's vessel"* (Psalm 2:9);
- he is an instrument of Rome, whose metallic symbol is iron.

This was true of the development of the Beast. The two-horned Beast from the Earth was *"like a lamb"* (Christ), but *"spoke like a dragon"* (pagan Rome).

Is it possible to identify the Man Child with one specific Roman emperor, Constantine, who 'Christianised' the Empire? While it is true that the change from paganism to Christianity occurred through Constantine's work, the symbol of the Man Child also incorporates the much longer development of a human government parading as if it were Christ's. This started in Constantine's day, but it also became a feature of the subsequent history of Rome.

The Beast with two horns

When the Beast's development is described in chapter 13, one phase is quite striking. The Beast that came up out of the earth, *"had two horns like a lamb and spoke like a dragon"* (Revelation 13:11). After the decline and fall of the Roman empire, the division between West and East was finalised when Charlemagne, king of the Franks, was crowned as Roman emperor on Christmas Day, AD800. At the same time Charlemagne restored the disgraced Pope, and united political and religious power in the West. Charlemagne started what became known as the Holy Roman Empire: ruled jointly by church and state. The two horns on the Beast of the Earth symbolise these twin powers, now exercised through a Beast that was really the old Dragon (pagan Rome) masquerading as a lamb – i.e., as if it was Christian.

The 18th century French author and philosopher Voltaire summed up the situation very cleverly when he wrote: *"This agglomeration which was called and which still calls itself the Holy Roman Empire was neither holy, Roman, nor an empire"* (Essai sur les Mœurs et l'Esprit des Nations, lxx).

Like a man

As the Beast developed, it was like the Man Child in the vision of Revelation 12 growing up into "a man". This important aspect of the Beast is shown both in Revelation and Daniel, where one of its horns had eyes *"like a man"* (Daniel 7:8). Gradually, as the Beast changed, power was concentrated in one of its horns, and this horn spoke blasphemously. In the final picture, the Beast is shown to be "**full** *of names of blasphemy"* (Revelation 17:3).

This development is also described in other parts of the Bible, where warnings are given about those who are opposed to God while still claiming to be 'Christian':

> *"Let no one deceive you by any means; for that day will not come unless the falling away comes first, and the man of sin is revealed, the son of perdition, who opposes and exalts himself above all that is called God or that is worshipped, so that he sits as God in the temple of God, showing himself that he is God."*
>
> (2 Thessalonians 2:3,4)

This fits exactly the picture Daniel was given of the horns on the Beast gradually coming under the control of one power that had features *"like a man"* (Daniel 7:8).

Two men

Two contrasting developments are therefore described in Revelation by the figure of a Man. First, God is calling out of the nations a people for His name. These people are encouraged to be Christlike in their ways; to be so united with him in mind and heart that they become *"like the Son of Man"* (Revelation 1:13). When Jesus returns, they will form the *"Perfect Man"* revealed in the opening Vision of Revelation. They are also the Bride of Christ, *"prepared as a bride adorned for her husband"* (21:2).

But at the same time as the Perfect Man is being developed, another Man is being formed: *"the Man of Sin"*. The Beast of human government eventually has **a man's** eyes and **a man's** mouth, yet he claims to be God, and *"deceives those who dwell on the earth"* (Revelation 13:14).

The *"Man of Sin"* rules during the present era. The *"Perfect Man"* will rule only when God's kingdom replaces the kingdom of men.

The first and second great earthquakes therefore describe significant changes in the Beast's career. The first earthquake marked the change from Pagan Rome to an empire that embraced Christianity. The second earthquake destroyed the connection between church and state, leaving the corrupt church as a sinister influence in the kingdoms of men. A different phase of the Beast's power is evident during the last judgement period in Revelation. These judgements fall on the seat of the Beast's power, as we shall see in the next chapter.

Seven last plagues

JUDGEMENTS ON THE THRONE OF THE BEAST

MANY changes occurred on the stage of human history after John received the Revelation. After the seven seal judgements on pagan Rome, and the seven trumpet judgements on 'Christianised' Rome, the once great empire was little more than a collection of different nations. Daniel foresaw this when he interpreted Nebuchadnezzar's dream of the great metallic image. The feet of the image were partly of iron and partly of clay: *"so the kingdom shall be partly strong and partly fragile"* (Daniel 2:42). Nebuchadnezzar was told that it would be *"in the days of these kings (that) the God of heaven will set up a kingdom which shall never be destroyed"* (verse 44).

Everything indicates therefore that this third sequence of judgements is the last before Jesus returns to establish God's kingdom. And this is confirmed in the Kingdom Visions in chapters 14 and 15. Significantly, there are two visions, because they introduce two distinct sections. One forms the prelude to the seven last plagues (chapter 14), and the other explains an aspect of Christ's work once he returns to earth.

The fall of Babylon

Chapter 14 is a vision of Jesus and the redeemed saints on mount Zion. They rejoice because of the wonderful news that *"Babylon is fallen, is fallen, that great city, because she has made all nations drink of the wine of the wrath of her fornication"* (14:8).

This is the first time in Revelation that the kingdom of men is called "Babylon". This shows that there is a special aspect to the kingdom in this last phase of its development that makes it particularly appropriate to be named after Nebuchadnezzar's idolatrous empire. The characteristic of ancient Babylon that was most offensive to God was its false religion. It was a counterfeit of the true religion, and therefore more inclined to deceive.

We should therefore expect the last phase of the kingdom of men to be dominated by a false religious system. Nor should it surprise us when it is this factor that holds together the different parts of the kingdom of men. Revelation 17 describes the downfall of Babylon, showing that the Beast (the kingdom of men) is ridden and controlled in this last phase by a drunken prostitute. The Woman of Revelation 12 has become so corrupt that this is the only fitting symbol that can describe her. What started as a faithful Christian church grew immoral through greed for power, riches and human glory.

The vision in Revelation 14 sounds a warning to the true followers of Jesus not to be deceived by this debased form of Christianity: *"If anyone worships the beast and his image, and receives his mark on his forehead or on his hand, he himself shall also drink of the wine of the wrath of God, which is poured out full strength into the cup of his indignation"* (14:9,10).

Peace on earth

The second Kingdom Vision prepares us for another future development: seven thunders. These are explained in the panel alongside. Together, the two visions of Revelation 14 & 15 prepare the ground for the last phase of judgements before Jesus returns: *"No one was able to enter the temple* (i.e., the kingdom) *till the seven plagues of the seven angels were completed"* (15:8). The objective of these plagues is finally to bring peace to the earth. This is described in the vision that introduces them in the following terms:

> *"A sea of glass mingled with fire, and (I saw) those who have the victory over the beast, over his image and over his mark and over the number of his name, standing on the sea of glass, having harps of God. They sing the song of Moses, the servant of God, and the song of the Lamb, saying: 'Great and marvellous are*

Seven thunders

The vision in chapter 15 shows us *"those who have the victory over the beast, over his image and over his mark and over the number of his name"* (15:2). They sing about the time when God's judgements are made manifest (verse 4). This introduces a new phase that is not fully described in Revelation. Back in chapter 10, John was told, *"Seal up the things which the seven thunders uttered, and do not write them"* (verse 4). It is strange in a book called The Revelation – i.e., about uncovering and explaining things that are hidden – to have part of its message sealed up and closed from view.

The book of Revelation is Jesus' message to John and to all his faithful followers. After his death and resurrection, Jesus ascended to heaven, where he waits for the appointed day when his Father will send him back to the earth to set up His kingdom. The message of Revelation was given to instruct Jesus' disciples in advance of the momentous events that would occur between his ascension to heaven and his return to the earth. When we come across a section that remains "sealed up", it is likely therefore to refer to events that Jesus will be able to reveal personally once he has returned – i.e., events that will occur when he comes back to set up God's kingdom.

But, accepting that we cannot know in detail about the "seven thunders", is there a general message to be learned about them? Thunders are used in the Bible to describe God's judgements on the enemies of His people. Hannah, in her prayer in 1 Samuel 2, said: *"The adversaries of the* LORD *shall be broken in pieces; from heaven he will thunder against them"* (verse 10).

We have already thought about the destruction of Jericho as a pattern for the book of Revelation and its message about Jesus overcoming the kingdom of men. But the overthrow of Jericho was only the beginning of the conquest of the Land. As the Apostle Paul said when he spoke in the synagogue in Antioch, *"when God had destroyed **seven** nations in the land of Canaan, he distributed their land to them by allotment"* (Acts 13:19). The "seven thunders" may therefore refer to the subduing of the kingdom once Jesus returns to the earth. The details of these campaigns did not need to be revealed to John, for Jesus will be back in the earth to tell his disciples about them face to face.

your works, Lord God Almighty! Just and true are your ways, O King of the saints!" (verses 2,3)

The Harlot and the Bride

The plagues affect the kingdom of men in its 'Babylon' phase – in other words, they occur specifically in response to the false and deceptive religious dimension of human government in its final and most perverse development. The contrast between Babylon, the corrupt church, and the Bride of Christ, his true church, is worth noting (see table on page 77).

The first four plagues, following the pattern of the first four trumpets, fall on "the earth", "the sea", "rivers and fountains of waters", and finally on "the sun". These each relate, as we have discovered, to the people and the rulers of the kingdom of men.

First plague

The first plague, upon "the earth", affects all who are in the Beast's kingdom and *"who had the mark of the beast and those who worshipped his image"* (Revelation 16:2). The plague brought a *"foul and loathsome sore"*. Like a running sore, the events that started with the second great earthquake gradually infected all the kingdom of the Beast. The previous dominance of a small ruling elite was removed, but those who were freed from that tyranny did not turn to God. The old system where power was held by a small select group was desperately corrupt. But the system that replaced it – power in the hands of the people themselves – was also corrupt, and just as ungodly.

Second and third plagues

The second and third plagues on *"the sea"* and the *"rivers and fountains of waters"* turned both of them so that they became

"The woman, drunk with the blood of the saints, and … of the martyrs of Jesus" (Revelation 17:6)

"as blood" (verses 3,4). This should remind us of God's plagues against Egypt when, through Moses, He was asking Pharaoh to release His people from bondage (Exodus 7:19). In both cases, the purpose is identical. God is bringing about the salvation of His people from oppression and tyranny by sending plagues on their oppressor.

Fourth plague

The fourth plague was directed at "the sun" (Revelation 16:8). As the brightest star in "the heavens", the sun represents the king or emperor. This indicated that attempts to reinstate a single empire over the territory of the former Roman Empire were to be frustrated. Nebuchadnezzar was shown that the kingdom of men immediately before the return of Christ would constitute a variety of powers that fail to act in a united way. Men arose, like Napoleon and Hitler, with visions of great empires lasting for a thousand years (did they get these ideas from the Book of Revelation?). As they neared their goal, catastrophe struck. They were like Icharus, the man in Greek mythology who flew too near the sun so that the wax holding his wings together melted. They too were *"were scorched with great heat"* (verse 9).

But still the ultimate objective was not accomplished: *"they blasphemed the name of God who has power over these plagues; and they did not repent and give him glory"* (verse 9).

Fifth plague

So the fifth plague was directed at *"the throne of the beast, and his kingdom became full of darkness"* (verse 10). With the plague upon the sun, the lights of the kingdom of men were extinguished, leaving the Beast's kingdom in darkness. Once again, it is like the plagues on Egypt, when Moses was told, *"Stretch out your hand toward heaven, that there may be darkness over the land of Egypt, darkness which may even be felt"* (Exodus 10:21). That was also the occasion when a difference was made between the Egyptians, who were plunged into darkness, and the children of Israel who *"had light in their dwellings"* (verse 23). The objective was the same, that the inhabitants of the earth and their rulers would learn that God is supreme.

Sixth plague

The sixth plague is in two parts. Remembering how the sixth trumpet showed the invasion of the Eastern Empire by the Turks, this power is now shown as drying up – the river Euphrates representing the territories of those who invaded and inhabited the Eastern portion of the Empire. According to Revelation 16:12, the Turkish power had to wane, *"so that the way of the kings from the east might be prepared"*. These kings "from the sun's rising" are the glorified followers of Jesus.

> **Kings from the East**
> The redeemed saints sing: *"You have made us kings and priests to our God; and we shall reign on the earth."*
> (Revelation 5:10)

Speaking of the day of his return, Jesus said about his faithful disciples that, *"The righteous will shine forth as the sun in the kingdom of their Father. He who has ears to hear, let him hear!"* (Matthew 13:43).

But there is also another aspect to the purpose of this plague. We know from other passages of scripture that the return of Jesus will also bring about the restoration of the kingdom to Israel (Acts 1:6). But the Land of Palestine was being trodden down by the Gentiles: first by the Romans, and then (as part of the trumpet judgements) by the Ottoman empire. The Turkish power had to decline if scattered Jews from all over the world were to have opportunity to return to Israel. There has to be a re-gathering of God's people to their land before Jesus returns from heaven to establish the Kingdom – even though Jews will return for economic reasons without believing in His promises.

This great regathering started in earnest at the beginning of the 20th century, and continued with renewed vigour immediately after the Second World War. This fulfilment of Bible prophecy gives confidence about other events foretold in God's word.

> **Unclean Spirits like frogs**
>
> A plague of frogs occurred in Egypt when Moses asked Pharaoh to release the Children of Israel (Exodus 8:1-6). They invaded everything. Frogs were worshipped in Egypt, yet they are repulsive creatures, known for mindless croaking.
>
> The "unclean spirits like frogs" have this same character. All who were infected by the frog-spirit were united by an unclean religion; all croak the same things.

SEVEN LAST PLAGUES

The Harlot		The Bride	
Babylon	17:5	Jerusalem	21:10
Sits on many waters	17:1	Stands on sea of glass	15:2
Commits fornication	17:2	A virgin	14:4
In the wilderness	17:3	In heaven	21:10
Sits on scarlet beast	17:3	Stands on Mount Zion	14:1
Names of blasphemy	17:3	Names of 12 tribes	21:12
Purple and scarlet	17:3,4	Clean white linen	19:8
Golden cup of abominations	17:4	Prayers of saints	8:3
Lives luxuriously	18:7	Great tribulation	7:14
Mystery	17:5	Mystery finished	10:7
Drunk with blood of saints	17:6	Pure river of water of life	22:1
Queen and no widow	18:7	Bride of the Lamb	21:9
Wails and laments	18:9	Sorrows no more	21:4
Her enemies rejoice over her	18:20	Rejoices with the Lamb	19:7
Burned with fire	18:9	Having the glory of God	21:11
Come out of her	18:4	Come	22:17

Unclean spirits

The second part of the sixth plague involves *"the kings of the earth and of the whole world, to gather them to the battle of that great day of God Almighty"* (Revelation 16:14). Something is going to cause the nations of the earth to withstand the rule of Christ. This is described in Revelation as *"unclean* (or devilish) *spirits like frogs coming out of the mouth of the dragon, out of the mouth of the beast, and out of the mouth of the false prophet"* (16:13).

The mouth of the Beast has always been its most significant feature. In Revelation 13:2 it was *"the mouth of a lion"*, i.e., it was Babylonish or religiously corrupted. In Daniel 7:8, it was *"speaking pompous words"*. And when this verse is quoted in Revelation 13:5, it adds that these pompous words were *"blasphemies"*. Before Jesus returns therefore, a spirit or atmosphere of blasphemy will pervade the whole earth. This message will proceed from the Beast (the powers occupying the territory of the former Western Roman Empire), from the Dragon (the old Eastern Empire that, for a time, preserved elements of pagan rule), and from the False Prophet (the representative of the corrupt religious system).

False Prophet

This is the first time the False Prophet is mentioned in Revelation, but warnings are made in other books of the Bible about false teachings. Jesus, for example, told his disciples to beware of *"false prophets, who come to you in sheep's clothing, but inwardly they are ravenous wolves"* (Matthew 7:15). In Revelation, the False Prophet was previously called *"the image of the beast"*. When the Empire's political power was waning, the false religious power worked first of all in the background, and then more openly to present an allegedly Christian organisation with its own private and corrupt plans. This power is called a "prophet", because it claims to speak on God's behalf; but its message is false, therefore it is called *"the **false** prophet"*.

The fact that this all-pervading spirit of blasphemy comes from the Beast, the Dragon *and* the False Prophet is further shown in Revelation 17 where the Beast is seen being controlled and ridden by the false church, shown as a gross prostitute. The blasphemies are therefore her teachings, and are promoted by political as well as by religious powers. She is so closely identified with the origin of blasphemy that she is called "*Babylon the Great*", and the beast she rides is "*full of names of blasphemy*". The effect of these "*unclean spirits like frogs*" is that the ten kings (who represent what is left of the kingdom of men, and who were symbolised by the ten horns on the Beast) "*are of one mind, and … give their power and authority to the beast*" (verse 13).

The kingdom of men unites
Remarkably, despite all that happened following the pouring out of the earlier plagues, when kings were deposed and kingdoms found it impossible to co-operate with each other, the sixth plague brings about a sudden unity of thought, such that they "*will make war with the Lamb, and the Lamb will overcome them, for he is Lord of lords and King of kings*" (verse 14).

This is where we are in the 21st century. It is at this time, when the kingdoms of the former Roman Empire are uniting and starting to speak with one voice, that Jesus says in Revelation 16:15, "*Behold, I am coming as a thief. Blessed is he who watches, and keeps his garments, lest he walk naked and they see his shame.*"

There is surely great significance in the fact that European unity in the past 50 years has been based on the Treaty of Rome (the foundation of European Unity, signed by six nations in 1957)!

Clearly, this antagonism to the truth of God's word is going to be a testing time for Jesus' followers. He asks them to "*keep their garments*", i.e., to hold fast to his teachings, assured of the salvation that is only available through his redeeming work.

At this crucial time in the development of God's purpose three dramatic things occur:

- The nations of the world gather together against the Lamb, Jesus and his followers.
- The third "great earthquake" shakes the earth like never before.
- The "Great City" is divided and Babylon falls.

This is so important that Revelation 17 and 18 describe the effect for all who live at that time. Normal life will be completely changed:

"*The great city Babylon shall be thrown down, and shall not be found any more. The sound of harpists, musicians, flutists, and trumpeters shall not be heard in you any more. No craftsman of any craft shall be found in you any more, and the sound of a millstone shall not be heard in you any more. The light of a lamp shall not shine in you any more, and the voice of bridegroom and bride shall not be heard in you any more. For your merchants were the great men of the earth, for by your sorcery all the nations were deceived.*" (Revelation 18:21-23)

Poster produced by the European Union to advertise the desire for unity.

Subduing the nations

EVENTS DURING THE MILLENNIUM

THE return of Jesus to the earth is not the end of God's purpose. When Jesus comes, he will find much ignorance about God, and opposition to his rule. The final section of Revelation explains how he will *"put an end to all rule and all authority and power"* and give the kingdom to his Father (1 Corinthians 15:24).

In common with the other sections of Revelation, this last section starts with a vision of the kingdom. We know that it is a vision of the final consolation, because a great multitude cries out, *"Alleluia! For the Lord God Omnipotent reigns!"* (Revelation 19:6). This great conclusion to God's purpose is also described as *"the marriage of the Lamb"*, and the whole review of events from John's day has told the story of how *"the Lamb's wife has made herself ready"* (verse 7).

The Millennium

John was also shown the return of Jesus as of a conquering hero coming to take the throne: *"I saw heaven opened, and behold, a white horse. And he who sat on him was called Faithful and True, and in righteousness he judges and makes war"* (verse 11). But the kingdom will not be conquered painlessly. Opponents of his coming who resist his rule will be overcome: *"He himself will rule them with a rod of iron. He himself treads the winepress of the fierceness and wrath of Almighty God"* (verse 15). This stage of God's purpose will take a thousand years to accomplish (see chapter on "Time periods", page 47). It is therefore sometimes called "the Millennium" (meaning a "thousand").

Jesus' opponents are, naturally, the descendants of the serpent: the Beast and the False Prophet and their armies (verses 19,20), and their destruction is certain and final – as certain and complete as when Sodom and Gomorrah were destroyed by fire and brimstone (verse 20, cp. Genesis 19:24).

But the Dragon (*"that serpent of old, who is the Devil and Satan"*, 20:2) was not destroyed with the Beast and the False Prophet – at least not at the same time. First of all, it is revealed that at Jesus' return the Dragon will be bound, so that his false teaching can no longer deceive the nations. In the language of Revelation 20:3, he is cast into *"the bottomless pit"*, which is sealed for a thousand years (see page 62).

The rule of Christ

This means that deception is totally removed from the earth for a thousand years. The rulership of Christ will be different from what has been previously experienced: *"He shall not judge by the sight of his eyes, nor decide by the hearing of his ears"* (Isaiah 11:3). It will be impossible to deceive Jesus, who *"had no need that anyone should testify of man, for he knew what was in man"* (John 2:25). Furthermore, the world itself will be instructed in the things of God, *"For out of Zion shall go forth the law, and the word of the L*ORD *from Jerusalem"* (Isaiah 2:3).

This work of instructing the population of the earth in God's ways will be delegated to the saints – the faithful followers of Jesus who (after the dead have been raised) will be accepted by him at the Judgement Seat. Speaking of these immortalised disciples of Jesus, John says, *"I saw thrones, and they sat on them, and judgment was committed to them"* (Revelation 20:4).

A thousand years seems a long time, but sin is so ingrained in mankind that it will take all that time to allow the full benefits of Jesus' rule to be felt over all the earth. There is an additional consequence of this long period of time. No one will be able to complain that God gives no opportunity for repentance: *"The Lord … is longsuffering toward us, not willing that any should perish but that all should come to repentance"* (2 Peter 3:9).

After 1,000 years

At the end of the thousand years, *"Satan will be released from his prison"* (Revelation 20:7). There is only one way this can happen, and that is if Jesus and the saints are no longer telling the world about God's word. Revelation 20:9 suggests that this is how it will happen, explaining that Jesus and his co-rulers retreat to *"the beloved city"*, where they await an attack from those involved in the final and great rebellion.

Just as will happen when Christ returns at the beginning of the thousand years, nations will gather together to battle as that period comes to an end. It will be a vain and futile exercise. How can an immortal Jesus (i.e., one who is not able to die) and his equally immortal disciples be overcome? Of course they can't. But the attack will reveal beyond all doubt those who will refuse to accept the Lord Jesus as their king, and they will all be destroyed suddenly and decisively: *"fire came down from God out of heaven and devoured them"* (Revelation 20:9).

This is the last and final act of the Dragon. Now called simply *"the devil"* (or false accuser, because of the continual persecution of Jesus' true followers), the Dragon will be completely destroyed, *"cast into the lake of fire and brimstone where the beast and the false prophet are"* (verse 10).

SUBDUING THE NATIONS 19

The effect of this last great rebellion will be to leave on the earth only two groups of people:

- Jesus and the immortal saints, and
- Mortal inhabitants who refused to join in the great revolt.

The last judgement

But during the thousand years there will also be many who die, even though life expectancy is likely to be extended during the reign of Christ (see Isaiah 65:20). Those who have learned about Jesus will be raised at the end of the thousand years to stand alongside those who are still alive: *"I saw the dead, small and great, standing before God, and books were opened. And another book was opened, which is the book of life. And the dead were judged according to their works, by the things which were written in the books"* (Revelation 20:12).

The thousand years starts with the judgement of Christ on those who are alive when he returns to the earth, and on those who died awaiting his coming; and he will grant immortality to those *"who are Christ's at his coming"* (1 Corinthians 15:23). It will end with him sitting once more in judgement, but this time on those who live (and die) during his thousand year reign. The righteous will be granted everlasting life, *"And anyone not found written in the book of life was cast into the lake of fire"* (verse 15).

As the Apostle Paul told believers in Corinth, *"The last enemy that will be destroyed is death"* (1 Corinthians 15:26), and Revelation confirms this:

"Then Death and Hades (the Grave) were cast into the lake of fire."
(Revelation 20:14)

REVELATION STUDY GUIDE

New Heaven and New Earth

GOD WILL BE "ALL IN ALL"

THE last section of the book of Revelation showed the Apostle John and his readers the situation at the end of the millennium when, as the Apostle Paul described it to believers in Corinth, God will be *"all in all"* (1 Corinthians 15:28). This requires the complete removal of the old order, where men and women appoint their own rulers and decide their own destiny. There has to be a *"new heaven"* – a different form of government, ordered according to divine principles. And there has to be a *"new earth"*, where the world's inhabitants are no longer affected by sin and death.

We saw in the vision that introduced the opening of the seven-sealed scroll the importance of the symbols of *"earth"* and *"heaven"* (page 51). When Peter wrote to believers in his day he confirmed that the followers of Christ have always looked *"for **new** heavens and a **new** earth in which righteousness dwells"* (2 Peter 3:13). This is the key to understanding God's promised future age: it will be an era characterised by righteousness, and inhabited by individuals who live wholly in accordance with God's will, as the Lord Jesus did throughout his life on earth.

Heavenly Jerusalem

This situation can only exist when sin and death have been removed completely from the earth, as we saw in the last chapter (page 79; Revelation 20:14). Jesus' faithful disciples, freed at last from the weakness of mortality, are true citizens of "heavenly Jerusalem" – Revelation's description of the complete community of believers who are united with God through the work of the Lord Jesus Christ.

But they are also described as Jesus' Bride, *"the Lamb's wife"* (21:9). One of the angels who brought the seven last plagues (surely the seventh?) called John to come and view the Lamb's wife, and what John saw was *"**the great city**, the holy Jerusalem, descending out of heaven from God, having the glory of God"* (verses 10,11). The organisation of the kingdom of men, previously described in Revelation as *"the great city"* (11:8; 16:19; 17:18; 18:10, etc.) has therefore been replaced by *"new heavens"*, a divine organisation coming *"from God"*.

This great city is the fulfilment of God's purpose with the inhabitants of the earth. The description of it is highly symbolic. The city describes all the individuals whose salvation is assured through the work of the Lord Jesus Christ, as the table below shows:

The Holy City, New Jerusalem	The Saints
Wall of jasper, clear as crystal and of pure gold free from imperfection or fault	The result of tried faith
12 Gates, made of a single pearl	Guarded by 12 angels named after Israel's 12 tribes
Called by the Gospel, the "pearl of great price" (Matthew 13:46)	And "the hope of Israel" (Acts 28:20)
12 Foundations adorned with precious stones	Named after the 12 apostles
As colours combine to produce clear, white light, the saints are united in Jesus	Through the apostolic preaching of the Gospel

The freedom and joy of the earth when it is finally released from the effects of sin and death is shown by the description of those who enter "the city":

"*The nations of those who are saved shall walk in its light, and the kings of the earth bring their glory and honour into it. Its gates shall not be shut at all by day (there shall be no night there). And they shall bring the glory and the honour of the nations into it.*"

(Revelation 21:24-26)

All nations healed

These final chapters emphasise the great healing that will be necessary before the world can expect God to dwell with men and women. The city contains:

A "*pure river of water of life*", because the word of God will flow from it unrestrained.

The "*tree of life*", producing fruit every month "*for the healing of the nations*".

The throne of God and of the Lamb – the centre of God's government.

Continual and unrestricted light – no darkness caused by sin.

The effect on the Apostle John of all the visions he saw was to cause him to worship the angel who brought Jesus' message. But he was told that all worship should be directed to God Himself who planned and revealed His purpose, and who continues to work towards its fulfilment.

John was told:

"*Do not seal the words of the prophecy of this book, for the time is at hand.*" (22:10)

It was important that the message of Revelation be widely distributed and read. It contains an urgent message for Jesus' followers: "**for the time is at hand**".

NEW HEAVEN AND NEW EARTH 20

An urgent message

This urgency is further emphasised by Jesus' own words: *"Behold, I am coming quickly, and my reward is with me, to give to every one according to his work"* (verse 12). Jesus invites his faithful followers to enter through the gates into the city. Only in *"New Jerusalem"* will there be life. Outside the city *"are dogs and sorcerers and sexually immoral and murderers and idolaters, and whoever loves and practices a lie"* (verse 15). The earth will be cleansed from all these ungodly activities during Jesus' 1,000-year reign.

The book of Revelation concludes with Jesus stressing the importance of his final message. He warns John about the danger of adding to it, or taking away from it. Those who try to add to it will be liable to the plagues it mentions. Those who take away from it will have their place in God's purpose taken away from them.

In Revelation 22 Jesus uses three different expressions to describe himself. Each of them is very informative:

> *"I am the Alpha and the Omega, the Beginning and the End, the First and the Last."* (verse 13)

This confirms that the whole purpose of God, right from the beginning, has been centred in Jesus. He was *"the Lamb slain from the foundation of the world"* (13:8).

> *"I am the Root and the Offspring of David ..."* (22:16)

Jesus confirms that the promises to the Jewish patriarchs all find their fulfilment in him. The Gospel was preached to Noah, Abraham, David, the Apostles – many people living both before and after the period of Jesus' ministry on earth.

> *"I am ... the Bright and Morning Star."* (verse 16)

Jesus brings new light – to the lives of individuals now who try to honour his work, but finally and completely to all the world when he reigns in his Father's kingdom.

"Even so, come, Lord Jesus!"

"The grace of our Lord Jesus Christ be with you all."

Amen

20 REVELATION STUDY GUIDE

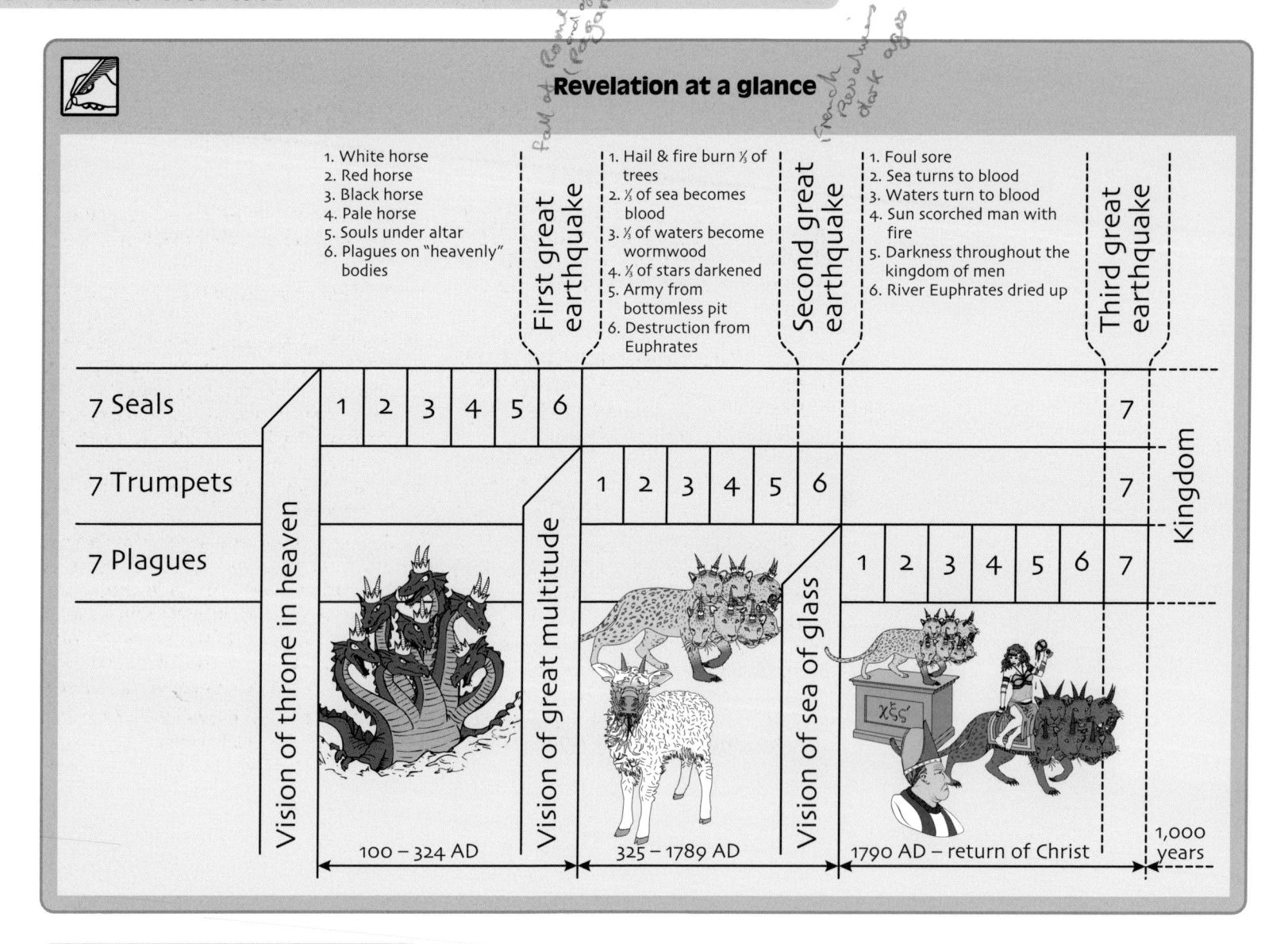

Revelation at a glance

Handwritten annotations: "Fall of Rome (end of Paganism)", "French Revolution", "dark ages"

	7 Seals	7 Trumpets	7 Plagues
Seals 1–6	1. White horse / 2. Red horse / 3. Black horse / 4. Pale horse / 5. Souls under altar / 6. Plagues on "heavenly" bodies		
First great earthquake			
Trumpets 1–6		1. Hail & fire burn ⅓ of trees / 2. ⅓ of sea becomes blood / 3. ⅓ of waters become wormwood / 4. ⅓ of stars darkened / 5. Army from bottomless pit / 6. Destruction from Euphrates	
Second great earthquake			
Plagues 1–6			1. Foul sore / 2. Sea turns to blood / 3. Waters turn to blood / 4. Sun scorched man with fire / 5. Darkness throughout the kingdom of men / 6. River Euphrates dried up
Third great earthquake			
7th / Kingdom	Seal 7	Trumpet 7	Plague 7

Timeline:
- Vision of throne in heaven — 100–324 AD
- Vision of great multitude — 325–1789 AD
- Vision of sea of glass — 1790 AD – return of Christ
- Kingdom — 1,000 years

86

Further reading

IF this Study Guide has whetted your appetite to learn more about the book of Revelation there are a number of other books that will help you explore its message more extensively.

1. *Interpreting the Book of Revelation,* by Alfred Nicholls concentrates on the approach taken to present details of God's unfolding purpose. The author explains the principles that should be followed to interpret the different aspects of the account. Not all of Revelation is covered in this book; as its title suggests, it concentrates only on how to interpret the message. However, in the process, some critical passages are explained in helpful detail.

2. *Notes on the Apocalypse,* by C.C. Walker is an extremely useful little work. In a very compressed form it applies the principles set out in the previously mentioned book, and explains each verse. Due to its short length, it does not commit a lot of space to explaining the method of interpretation that is followed.

3. *Thirteen Lectures on the Apocalypse,* by Robert Roberts. As the title suggests, this is basically a transcript of lectures that were first delivered before an audience of interested people. They are therefore very readable, and lead readers through the book section by section, explaining both the message of Revelation, and how it can be interpreted.

4. For serious students who want further information about how the book of Revelation expands on earlier scriptures in explaining the unfolding purpose of God, Part III of *Elpis Israel* by John Thomas is a very useful introduction to the author's much longer work, *Eureka*.

All the above are available from the publishers of this Study Guide.